RELEASING
THE
MONEY ANOINTING

BY
CHARLES WINBURN

FOREWORD BY
DR. MARK HANBY

Releasing the Money Anointing

Charles Winburn may be contacted at:
5766 Willow Cove Drive
Cincinnati, OH 45239
(513) 542-9932
E-mail: CEWinburn@yahoo.com
Web Site: Churchincollegehill.org

Creative Services and Publishing by:
CSN Books
1975 Janich Ranch Court
El Cajon, CA 92019
CSNbooks.com
(Toll free) 1-866-6184

FOREWORD

I had never met Charles Winburn; he knew me only by pictures on my books and tapes. So, our first meeting was one of those unlikely "coincidences" that we later recognized as a sovereign work of the Holy Spirit.

I had gone to Gold's Gym at 6:30 a.m. to torture my already well-worn body and was hanging up my car keys, when I overheard someone say, "He looks just like him...I think that might be him." I turned to see two gentlemen looking directly at me; they had followed me into the gym. Charles Winburn and a fellow pastor were delighted when I introduced myself, and seemed perfectly content to jog along for the next hour while we became better acquainted—our conversation literally was carried on in short "pants."

We had a common friend in one of my ministry sons, Jim Becton of Houston, Texas, and definitely had common interests in our desire to grow in Kingdom understanding. And now, here we were in Destin, Florida! Charles resides, and is an apostle, in Cincinnati, Ohio, and was attending a ministry conference in Santa Rosa Beach. Linda and I were taking some time away from our Tennessee ranch, desperately seeking answers to a most pressing multi-million dollar Kingdom business challenge. Meeting each other seemed so unlikely that we agreed to get together later to see what God was really up to.

In subsequent meetings, we discussed a broad array of Kingdom subjects: The Kingdom Relating to the Church (The Voice Behind Me), The Rest of God "The Like as Principle," The Three-Dimensions of Glory, The Third Dimension of Grace, The Seventh Day of God, etc. At one point in our conversation, Charles Winburn mentioned that he had authored and was finalizing the manuscript of a new book entitled, *Releasing the Money Anointing*. My immediate reaction was to humorously retort, "Maybe you could pray for me to receive a money anointing. I'm desperate for divine intervention concerning Kingdom finances." I actually had only five days to acquire $125,000 or face a potential multi-million dollar catastrophe involving many of my precious Christian friends.

I had no idea that this apostle of God took me seriously. I was amazed that within hours of our conversation, and Charles Winburn's obviously anointed interaction, I received the thousands of dollars that I needed. As I write this Foreword, the business that I spoke of has completely turned around, and the burden has been lifted from me and others who were seemingly hopelessly involved.

What we had considered a possible huge loss has become a very promising blessing! Charles Winburn truly stirred up and helped to activate the release of the money anointing in my life. I am still amazed at the suddenness with which it all took place.

I have read many books regarding Biblical economics and financing the end time harvest. However, when I read *Releasing the Money Anointing*, I stepped into a whole new learning experience–a true revelation of releasing money in the third dimension. This book defines more clearly than any other I have read our link to that dimension of prosperity and blessing through resting in God.

In *Releasing the Money Anointing*, Charles Winburn prepares the mind for an abundance in the third dimension of grace. He teaches how to obtain money without working hard for it. He teaches us how money comes "through us" instead of "to us" so we can be a blessing to others. So then, the money anointing is part of our generational wealth. This book helps us recognize that we are indeed the wealth of God.

When I think of financial blessings, I think of the anointing as being in the second dimension of grace, the Church. However, when I read this book, I sensed a heavenly deposit in the third dimension of grace, a true Kingdom anointing.

I am told that there are over 400,000 churches in America. Many of these churches, pastors, bishops or apostles endeavor to teach their people how to receive financial blessings. I believe this book could be the answer, helping to prepare people of God for abundance and favor that can be transferred to help fund the apostolic work in the earth.

Finally, this revolutionary book, *Releasing the Money Anointing*, puts money in the right perspective by teaching that money is the purpose, but giving it away to bless others is the destiny. This is also a great book for business people and those who spend their time in the marketplace.

Releasing the Money Anointing has definitely come in the right season and at the right time for God's people. Not only will you want to read it over and over again, but you should encourage your pastor, friends, spiritual leaders and business leaders to do the same.

Dr. Mark Hanby
Best-selling author and
Founder of
Mark Hanby Ministries

TABLE OF CONTENTS

GIVING HONOR
WHERE HONOR IS DUE

It is Carl H. Lindner's life (a born-again believer) of giving that inspired me to write this book, and I honor him on this page. Mr. Carl H. Lindner is an uncommon seed giver. He has given away millions of his wealth to bless many people. In the last decade he has given away over 200 million dollars to charities. It has always been my desire to become an uncommon sower of finances into peoples' lives like Carl H. Lindner.

Carl H. Lindner's family founded United Dairy Farmers in 1940 as a single storefront selling dairy products. Their first day sales amounted to $8.28.

Today, Mr. Lindner is Chairman of the Board, Chief Executive Officer, Founder and principal shareholder of American Financial Group Inc., a diversified financial holding company principally engaged in property-casualty and life insurance. He is also the largest shareholder of Provident Financial Group. The combined assets of these two companies are $30 billion. Carl H. Lindner is also the owner of the Cincinnati Reds baseball team. My dear friend doesn't have a lofty education, but he has a huge anointing for money, wealth, abundance, and wisdom. This 84-year-old man calls me on a regular basis just to see how I am doing. Not only does he give away his money, but he gives his life away to others. Mr. Carl Lindner most recently decided to sell Provident Bank. About the time this book is launched around the world, Provident Financial Group will be sold to the Cleveland-based National City Corp. Under the dynamic leadership of Carl Lindner, Provident Bank has been a great blessing to more than one-half million customers.

3

My friend, Carl H. Lindner, has given so much of his spirit, soul and wealth to bless so many people in the earth.

I want to encourage you, the reader, to become an uncommon financial seed giver to others. This book will help put you into a position so that you will be able to generate more revenue or income with a view toward blessing the apostolic work of God in the Earth.

THE LATE BISHOP WILLIAM JAMES

I would also like to honor the late Bishop William James Legacy, who was a spiritual father to me.

Bishop William James was the presiding bishop of the Church of God in Christ, Ohio North Jurisdiction, and former member of the General Board of the Church of God in Christ Inc.

Under Bishop Williams James, I learned how to tithe, give offerings and sow financial seeds toward the work of God. Bishop William James had a gift of giving, and I watched him financially bless so many people that it inspired and activated me to learn the principles of giving. I am now able to bless so many people by giving and making available this book on releasing the money anointing.

Under Bishop William James, I received an impartation in the financial realm and also discovered that I had this same type of gift.

Finally, Bishop James taught me about sanctification and holiness. I appreciated the instruction, correction, and rebuke he brought to my life and, as a result, I learned how to submit to both spiritual and natural authorities.

It is also my prayer that after you read this book that the anointing will open up the floodgates of money so you can be a blessing to others.

WHO CAN BENEFIT

From Reading
Releasing the Money Anointing?

Corporations

All employers should require their employees to read *Releasing the Money Anointing*. This book can help small and big businesses to increase profitability by changing the thoughts of their employees, teaching them to view money in a different way. Watch the profits increase in your company when your employees see money differently.

Colleges and Universities

All college and university students, especially students in the School of Business and Economics, should read *Releasing the Money Anointing* as a "required reading" textbook. The truths in this book will help students become better employees after graduation.

Churches

Releasing the Money Anointing will help churches increase their financial giving, and help churches expand their donor base and stewardship programs. This book should be required reading for those going into ministry or Christian education.

Community Development Corporations

Members of the CDC's who are trying to generate revenue for their corporations will help expand the financial minds of their leaders and volunteers as they learn how to release the money anointing. It will be great reading!

Foundations, Alumni Associations and Tax Exempt Organizations

This book will help all corporate fund-raisers to think

differently about how they see themselves in the fund–
raising market. The principles taught in this book will help
them expand their donor base and increase the amount of
donations their organizations receive.

Banks, Financial Institutions and Stock Brokers

Releasing the Money Anointing will help bankers and
loan officers take the stress out of money by learning new
principles to generate loans, and by learning how to identify
and attract the right kind of customers. This book can also
be passed on to these same customers who will be securing
loans and making long term investments in these financial
institutions.

PREFACE

Interconnecting Truths

Releasing the Money Anointing focuses on receiving spiritual money. It's money that you first see, and then ultimately receive, by walking in faith. This book is built on interconnecting truths. You cannot write a book of this magnitude without talking about other principles such as divine health, divine healing, mind health, self-talk and adjusting your thought life.

All of these divine principles *interconnect* to make the whole. In other words, there are other interconnecting truths in this book that holistically bring together many concepts in helping the reader to release the money anointing in his or her life.

I honestly believe that there is no book in the world like this one!

Releasing the Money Anointing systematically activates the anointing in your life as you read it, chapter-by-chapter. It is designed, as you read it, to bring you into what you read as you apply the principles. This book is a very unique, witty invention of the anointing of God.

There is only one anointing, but it manifests itself in four dimensions or operations. There is only one God, who expresses Himself in three distinct personalities. There are not three gods in the Godhead, but only one God. The Father in creation, the Son in redemption, and the Holy Spirit who leads us into all truth. The Father, Son and Holy Ghost make up the Godhead.

Jesus said, *"I and the Father are one."* The Rhema word or Rhema anointing is also an expression or dimension of God. According to John 1:1-2:

In the beginning was the Word, and the Word was with God and the Word was God. The same was in the beginning with God.

There is a powerful anointing in the Godhead. This book helped search it out. We separated, for clarification, the Godhead into three distinct personalities or dimensions in this book.

In the Godhead, you can see the power within the power of God. The glory within the glory of God, the presence within the presence of God, the anointing within the anointing of God.

This book will focus on the anointing within the anointing of the Godhead. We look at the Father's anointing, the Son's anointing, the Holy Spirit's anointing, and the anointing from the Word of God, which I call "the Rhema anointing."

All of these distinct anointings are from the One source of the anointing, the Godhead. Learning how to release the anointing from the Godhead is key to walking in all that God has promised us in His Word, whether divine health, prosperity, wisdom, money, or abundance.

ABOUT THE AUTHOR

Charles Winburn is founder of the "Encampment"—the Church in College Hill, in Cincinnati, Ohio. The new "Encampment" is a Biblical training camp that focuses on discipleship training with a view toward helping people in their transition into the Kingdom of God.

Charles Winburn also serves on the Ohio Civil Rights Commission, appointed by Governor Bob Taft in 2001.

Charles is married to Coleen Winburn, and they have four children: Charles Winburn III (Carlos), 27; Charlene, 17; Charity, 12; and Joseph Charles, 7.

One hundred percent of the proceeds from this book will be used to fund the New Prayer Center and new "Encampment." Your donation of $18.95 is tax deductible.

INTRODUCTION

I have observed through the years that nothing in the Bible seems to cause more confusion and frustration than the greatly misunderstood area of God's financial principles. The Body of Christ has experienced a myriad of teachings on this subject, some greatly contradictory. On one hand, some teach that wealth interferes with God's plan, and it is far better to be poor. On the other, some feel that God is no more than a heavenly bank account that we can tap into whenever we desire, claiming the material things we want for our lives.

In this book, I have shared what the Holy Spirit has revealed to me as I have prayed and studied on this important subject for twenty years. As you read *Releasing the Money Anointing*, I pray that the same Holy Spirit will reveal to you the truth of these words, and then empower you to apply God's principles in your life to receive His anointing in your finances.

You have been anointed to receive money. Money is not anointed...you are anointed. This book will teach you how to release this anointing that will attract others to financially bless you so you can bless others with money and materials. You will become an answer to someone else's prayer, and help someone else reach their divine destiny by blessing them financially. And, you will initiate a greater financial blessing into your life by reading this book.

Charles Winburn

CHAPTER ONE

Stop the Elevator Ride in Your Finances!

This book takes you on an incredible spiritual journey that teaches you how to biblically release your money and wealth into the Kingdom of God and be a blessing to people. More importantly, it teaches you how to position yourself to reap the financial harvest God wants you to receive as you walk in and experience the fascinating realm of God's finances.

Get ready!

God wants to tell you something through this book that He could not tell you before.

God wants to get money to you that He was not able to get to you before you read this book.

***Releasing the Money Anointing* is a seed being planted in you right now. This seed is going to break out and break loose on you by releasing the prosperity you so deserve in your spirit, soul and body.**

Money Answers All Things

The Bible says in Ecclesiastes 10:19, "that money answers all things." I believe Solomon was describing "all things" as both tangible or inanimate objects.

Money will answer all external things such as:

1. Purchasing houses, land, real estate, and cars
2. Pays for medical bills such as a heart or kidney transplant.

3. Supports the Apostolic work of the Church.
4. Pays for Christian television.
5. Supports college educations.
6. Supports Apostolic missionaries.
7. Provides financial gifts to help others meet their goals.
8. Pays the salaries and provides compensation for employees.
9. Creates financial capital for a business or a corporation.

There are some things, however, that money cannot buy:

Joy, peace and righteousness in the Holy Ghost.
The God-kind of happiness.
The anointing of the Lord.
The presence of God.
Grace and mercy.
Salvation.
Tears of joy and weeping before God in brokenness.
Love.
Faith.
Hope.

You will not know if you are free from the control of money unless you give it away to others without conditions.

Erase Your Past

To get money to you, God must first erase your past! Did you know that all you have done this last year, and all you have done throughout your life, is now erased in God's eyes? He overlooks every fault, every financial failing you may have made, and He is ready to start you off with a clean slate.

As far as the east is from the west, so far hath he removed our transgressions from us.

(Psalm 103:12)

This is the dawning of a new day, a new anointing! This is His day for a new start, for new beginnings in your life!

God is ready to tell you something He could not tell you before because you had too much junk in your life to hear what He wanted to say!

In this book, you will experience a defining moment for your financial breakthrough.

Many of you reading this book have faithfully given your tithes and offerings to God for His work here on earth. You have given to the neighborhood Christian school, to the television evangelist, to help the church drug and alcohol program, but in your heart of hearts you have wondered, "Lord, it seems as though I am planting but I am not reaping any of Your promised breakthroughs in my finances."

Are you one of those who have given faithfully to God, yet nothing seems to be happening in your finances?

The windows of heaven do not seem to open and pour out a financial blessing too big for you to contain.

To begin to reverse that curse and release God's financial flow into your life, there are a few truths that you must first accept.

Financial Truth # 1:

<u>When your money has stopped and is not flowing back to you, something is happening to hinder God's Word</u>.

The key to this truth is to determine why money is not flowing back into your life. Your cry is, "Lord, why is it that I return my tithes, give my love offerings, and keep giving and giving, but money does not seem to flow to me on a regular basis? Lord, why is it that the revenue streams are

17

not there regularly? Oh, every now and then I receive a financial breakthrough for a few weeks, but then, a few months later, it seems like my funds have evaporated. I am back in the same old place–broke again. **My finances feel like an elevator, up and down, up and down.** Lord, why do my finances keep going back and forth?"

As the Lord has dealt with me on this subject, I am convinced He wants to stop the elevator ride in your finances so you can begin to experience a *constant flow* of finances. I am further convinced that God wants you to have a constant flow of money and revenues coming into your life *without any struggle* on your part.

Not only does God want to pour His financial blessings into your life - believe it or not - He has already done it for you!

This book was written for the simple purpose of helping you to learn and apply the biblical principles that will unlock God's financial blessing and flow them into your life.

Financial Truth # 2:

Give your money as an 'uncommon seed' so your money can consistently start flowing back to you to help establish the Kingdom of God or an apostolic work on the earth.

Releasing the Money Anointing teaches you how to honor God by releasing your money to God and man to unlock the process where God and man begin to flow it back into your life. Your money anointing will be released as you apply the biblical principles in this book in your own life.

You are important to God, and as shocking as it may sound to some, *God does not need your money!* You need money, not God. But, because you are important to God, He knows that if you do not have money, you cannot meet your needs and help fulfill God's purposes by helping others, and by financing the works of God on the Earth.

Financial Truth # 3:

<u>God wants all of His people to have money flowing to them on a consistent basis to be a blessing to others</u>.

Imagine...God's promise for your finances, and His anointing to receive that promise, are already in your life! As you learn how to release that anointing, then money will flow into your life.

God wants every person reading this book to have money flowing to them on a consistent basis.

Now, I am not just writing about money coming in through your job or business. God wants you to receive over and above these areas and experience a literal overflow–so much that you cannot contain it. **It will come from sources you never realized or expected...** money coming from your job is for seed sowing. The big money you receive will come from your seed sowing.

The Bible does promise (even though most do not know how to unlock the promise), that:

> *Give, and it shall be given unto you; good measure, pressed down, and shaken together, and running over, shall men give into your bosom.*
>
> (Luke 6:38,a)

As you grasp and apply God's financial principles, men and women in your life who know you will be coming to you with their petitions, knowing you have been financially empowered by God to help establish the Kingdom of God. God knows your heart, and He knows that He can trust you with His wealth–that you will be a good steward of what He flows into your life.

Some of you reading this book might be wondering, "Charles Winburn, why another book about money?"

Because money is very important to the Kingdom of God. As a matter of fact, money is at the top of His list of blessings, because even salvation is linked to finances. You see, the word for "salvation" is "soteria" which means "safety, security, health and prosperity." I also heard Dr. Creflo Dollar link the words "soteria", salvation and prosperity together Your *complete* salvation involves not just the spiritual realm, but also a state of prosperity where you have the riches of God's Kingdom and the material things you need to assist you here on Earth, including money. Those who say money is not that important to them are not telling the whole truth. If they lie about money, what else will they lie about?

The Kingdom of heaven is like a merchant man seeking godly pearls (Matthew 13:45-46). A merchant man is involved in buying and selling. You need godly pearls or money to buy and sell. Jesus has no problems with godly pearls or money. The Kingdom of God involves the circulation of money.

To begin your transformation that will unlock His anointing into your life, I pray you read this book over and over until you receive the revelation and impartation into your spirit. Once it sinks deep into your spirit, you will then begin to walk it out, even subconsciously, in all you do because now the Spirit of the Lord is moving you into the areas where you ought to go.

Nine Spiritual Principles

Flee also youthful lusts: but follow righteousness, faith, charity, peace, with them that call on the Lord out of a pure heart.

But foolish and unlearned questions avoid, knowing that they do gender strifes. And the servant of the Lord must not strive; but be gentle unto all men, apt to teach, patient...

(II Timothy 2:22-24)

The Apostle Paul covers nine important principles with his spiritual sons. In the unfolding revelation of this book, you will grow to appreciate each of these vital areas of growth as you handle money.

Principle # 1:
"Flee also youthful lusts."

Principle # 2:
Follow righteousness.

Principle # 3:
Avoid foolish questions.

Principle # 4:
A servant must not strive.

As you learn to *Release the Money Anointing*, you will not need to strive for a position or hierarchy to receive it! The money anointing will be easy for you because the anointing will break loose in you. All God needs is a little mustard seed faith to break loose in your life His financial anointing like it never has broken before!

Principle # 5:
Be gentle unto all men.

Principle # 6:
Be apt to teach.

Principle # 7:
Be patient (consistent).

Strive to be consistent in your life, and try to eliminate huge mood swings. Too many people have moods that swing dramatically up and down depending upon how they feel, or what someone has said to them. We must strive to be consistent in our moods so that we will witness God's presence in our lives by our stable manner.

Beloved, I pray that you may prosper in every way and [that your body] may keep well, even as [I know] your soul [emotions] keeps well and prospers.
(3 John 2, Amplified)

The main hindrance to receiving your money anointing, your materials, your divine health is due to your focus on yourself. You must clearly see *yourself*. One man told me, "Brother Charles, I love your ministry and this fellowship, but I have one problem with you." "What is it?" I asked. The answer shocked me. "You make me see myself, and I do not like to see or deal with myself."

The truth is, God can only use us and bless us as we see ourselves clearly, and determine to free ourselves from sin and deception.

Principle # 8:
In meekness, instructing those who oppose themselves.

Is it possible that by opposing yourself you do not have a financial, material or divine health release in your life? You keep returning your tithes and giving your offerings to God, but there is more to the financial anointing issue than that. The tithes and offerings are a method to get something unlocked, but they are not *the* source.

The source you need is the anointings! The anointing of Shemen (God in action), the anointing of Christos (Christ in action), the anointing of Pneuma (Spirit in action), and the Rhema of the anointing (Word in action).

And, the reason the anointing is not released is because you are looking at yourself; your focus is too much about you.

Principle # 9::
People are always defending themselves.

It is time to just shut up and be quiet. It does not matter who is right or wrong. The more time you spend on yourself (secretly loving yourself), the less time you have available for the anointing to flow in your life. Stop pampering yourself–it stops the flow of the anointing.

Get this: although you return your tithes and give big offerings to God, you can still be broke all the time until you decide to exchange self-consciousness with a God-consciousness. Think about God. You are too earthly; it is time for you to be heavenly. It is time to think about Him.

Satan Is Not Your Problem

Ask yourself, "What am I doing that is stopping my money from coming in?" Then let the Holy Spirit adjust you to flowing in Godly attitudes. Satan even runs from people in the church with bad attitudes. When demons run away from you, you are really in trouble.

You keep blaming everything on the devil, but the devil is not causing your problem...you are causing the problem! He knows what he is doing, but you do not know what you are doing. When you mess up, you blame it on the devil. "Well, the devil made me kiss that woman." The devil made me look at him and do those things."

Leave the devil alone! He's not your problem. He was defeated on the cross over 2,000 years ago! You create your own devils when you live in a sinful state.

Opposing yourself will hinder your financial release, your material release, your divine health release. Sowing to the flesh is opposing your spiritual life. Every time you sow to the flesh, you oppose your spiritual life. Sowing to the Spirit will release your spirit-life to receive the anointing of God.

Are You Frustrating the Holy Spirit?

One day you can be in the Spirit and the next moment you can be in the flesh. That is why the Apostle Paul told Timothy to be patient, to be consistent. One day you are sowing in the Spirit, the next day you are sowing in the flesh. God wants to use your vessel, and you are sending the Holy Spirit the wrong message, so the Holy Spirit does not know what to do. The Holy Spirit says, "I'm just going to stop trying to operate in that person's life. I can't flow in that person's life because they keep sending me the wrong message or a double message."

Do you keep frustrating the Holy Spirit, hindering the anointing of God that is already in you as a son of God? **That's right...your anointing is already there! You have a reservoir of the anointing already in you, but it cannot be released to bring about manifestations,** to bring about your finances, your materials and your health because you keep frustrating the anointing of God.

Somewhere in your life you have hindered the work, the anointing of God. You have said to yourself, "Why do they want to stop me? They just do not want me to get ahead." No man can stop you from going where God wants you to go.

It is not about affirmative action or quotas. Greater is He that is in me than He who is in the world!

You poor thing. You ought to be ashamed of yourself. You are poor, can't even balance your checkbook, yet you call yourself, "more than a conqueror." With no money?

You can oppose yourself in spirit, soul and body.

Think God-thoughts

You are an agent of God!

God does not sit around and think your thoughts. To communicate with God, speak to Him by the Spirit.

> *God is a Spirit, and they that worship must worship Him in Spirit and truth.*
>
> (John 4:24)

This book was also written to help you break out from your poverty prison and obtain greater money. Your lack of money has kept you in a financial prison, but now is the time to experience financial freedom. God wants to flow the money into your life to fix the roof, to buy a bigger home (if you need one), to pay ALL of your bills.

Aren't you tired of trying to balance a bare-bones budget?

Do you want more than enough so you can give from your God-given abundance, an "uncommon seed," to somebody else?

The Mind and Thoughts of God

The word "thought" is a bad word to most people. It intimidates most people because the word challenges us to use our minds. Someone (author unknown) once said,

"Watch your thoughts for they become your words.
"Choose your words, for they become actions.
"Understand your actions, for they become habits.
"Study your habits, for they will become your character.
"Develop your character, for it becomes your destiny."

For those who have not yet trained their mind in thought development, you might want to consider enrolling in a thought development training program because *Releasing the Money Anointing* will not help you without the proper training. You must learn to take responsibility for your own thoughts if you are going to properly apply the principles in this book.

You must become disciplined with your thoughts.

Thoughts are everything.

You shall have your thoughts just like you shall have your words (read Mark 11:23). Your thoughts are formed into words, and then your words are communicated consciously, or through self-talk, to your will, emotions or intellect which makes up your mind.

God has a mind...the mind of God.

And they put him in ward, that the mind of the LORD might be shewed them.

(Leviticus 24:12)

God has thoughts.

For I know the thoughts that I think toward you, saith the LORD, thoughts of peace, and not of evil, to give you an expected end.

(Jeremiah 29:11)

Christ has a mind.

For who hath known the mind of the Lord, that he may instruct him? But we have the mind of Christ.

(1 Cor. 2:16)

Christ has thoughts.

Let this mind be in you, which was also in Christ Jesus:

(Philippians 2:5)

The Holy Spirit has a mind, the mind and thoughts of the Spirit.

And he that searcheth the hearts knoweth what is the mind of the Spirit, because he maketh intercession for the saints according to the will of God.

(Romans 8:27)

God has a body, and we are the body of Christ in the earth.

God is thought; Christ is thought; the Holy Spirit is thought. The Godhead communicates to us through our renewed mind or thoughts. We have a spirit, soul and body.

And the very God of peace sanctify you wholly; and I pray God your whole spirit and soul and body be preserved blameless unto the coming of our Lord Jesus Christ.

(1 Thessalonians 5:23)

You need the two-edged sword of God to pierce your soul in order that your thoughts are made pure. Below are three primary Scriptures that solidify this truth.

For the word of God is quick, and powerful, and sharper than any two-edged sword, piercing even to the dividing asunder of soul and spirit, and of the joints and marrow, and is a discerner of the thoughts and intents of the heart.

(Hebrews 4:12)

Finally, brethren, whatsoever things are true, whatsoever things are honest, whatsoever things are just, whatsoever things are pure, whatsoever things are lovely, whatsoever things are of good report; if there be any virtue, and if there be any praise, think on these things.

(Philippians 4:8)

I beseech you therefore, brethren, by the mercies of God, that ye present your bodies a living sacrifice, holy, acceptable unto God, which is your reasonable service. And be not conformed to this world: but be ye transformed by the renewing of your mind, that ye may prove what is that good, and acceptable, and perfect, will of God.

(Romans 12:1-2)

God first communicates to you through your thoughts. When your thoughts are right, then God will speak to your recreated human spirit. When your thoughts are right, you will be able to rule and reign over your human body and take dominion in every aspect of life such as spiritual, financial, mental and material.

When your mind is renewed, you are in the perfect will of God. Conversely, when your thoughts are not right, you are not in the will of God. There are many in the Body of Christ who are doing the work of God outside the will of God.

The will of God is a renewed mind or thought life. The will of God is, "I and the Father are one." You are not going to be one with the Father with a crazy thought life.

The Work of God

The anointing is going to help you to the degree of your renewed thought life. The Holy Ghost is going to help you to the degree of your renewed thoughts in God. The glory of God is going to flow through you to the degree you renew your thought life.

The gifts of God will flow through you, the manifestations of the Spirit will flow in your life, your prayers are only going to be empowered to the degree that you possess and walk in a renewed thought life.

The talents of God + bad thoughts = crazy results! The power of God cannot work in your life when hindered by your bad thoughts.

Some people think that everything is going to be alright if they pray and fast. Here's a shocking but true spiritual fact: You can fast and pray and not get any results because your thoughts are not changed! Your praying and fasting will be in vain. Your prayers can be hindered because of your thoughts. For example, if a husband and wife's thoughts are not right, God will not answer their prayers according to I Peter 3:7. Your thoughts are your faith. Positive thoughts are faith toward God. Negative thoughts are faith towards self and the devil. You and the devil become one.

> *Likewise, ye husbands, dwell with them according to knowledge, giving honour unto the wife, as unto the weaker vessel, and as being heirs together of the grace of life; that your prayers be not hindered.*
>
> (1 Peter 3:7)

> *Thou will keep in him perfect peace, whose mind is stayed on thee because he trusteth in thee.*
>
> (Isaiah 26:3)

This scripture does not apply to everyone. What kind of mind will be kept in perfect peace? It's only the renewed mind that will enjoy this perfect peace (Romans 12:2). Get your mind renewed or transformed first, and then you will enjoy perfect peace.

> *For as he thinketh in his heart, so is he: Eat and drink, saith he to thee; but his heart is not with thee.*
> (Proverbs 23:7)

> *For I know the thoughts that I think toward you, saith the LORD, thoughts of peace, and not of evil, to give you an expected end.*
> (Jeremiah 29:11)

According to *Marriage Partnership* Magazine, approximately 51 million Americans have some form of mental disorder that links backs to some negative thought pattern one way or another in their lives. Major depression hits 9.1 million people each year; generalized anxiety attacks 4 million people each year; obsessive compulsive disorder hinders 3.9 million people each year; panic disorders impact 2.4 million lives each year; schizophrenia impacts 2 million people each year; and bipolar (manic depressive disorders) effect the lives of 2 million people each year.

Clearly, how we think impacts how we live!

Two Types of Thought Stimuli

There are two types of thought I want to deal with here.

The first involves <u>thought development as a lifestyle</u>. That means it operates from a perspective of faith. It means building a life of faith toward God, minute-by-minute. It means constantly changing of your thoughts, moment-by-moment. A thought–driven life is a destiny–driven life, built on the confidence that you shall have what you ultimately think and say.

Thought development as a lifestyle is a positive lifestyle, although not necessarily a concept of positive thinking. It's possible to use the concept of positive thinking only when you desire to be positive for a certain situation or circumstance, but then revert back to negative thinking in other circumstances. Many people I know who once employed the concept of "positive thinking," to achieve a victory or two in their lives, reverted again to negativity. Positive thinking is used by most people in what I call "situational thinking"–they turn it on or off like a hot or cold water faucet depending upon the situation. You use positive thinking only when you need to do it. Positive thinking is not what I am talking about as a means to change your life. I am talking about a *lifestyle* of renewing your mind daily in the Word of God.

Metamorphosis of the mind is thought development that includes the following processes: change the thoughts, fashion the thoughts, form the thoughts, and then transfigure the thoughts. Every day you must go through a process of renewing, cleaning and preserving Godly thoughts.

The "After" People

Thought Reactionary Development is a life built upon positive thinking that comes and goes (like fear and panic). It is very difficult for this group of thinkers to maintain peace of mind and joy over a long period of time. The people in this group are those who react to problems, challenges and life on a daily basis. They have not properly trained their minds and their thoughts, so their lives tend to go up and down emotionally.

They react and overreact.

This group of people are not against change, but only attempt to change when a crises hits their lives. They are known as the "after people." Typically, after they are diagnosed with a heart attack or high cholesterol, they are ready to change their lifestyles. After they are diagnosed with obesity, they are ready to get off fatty foods, exercise and change their diet. After they are diagnosed with lung cancer, they are ready to stop smoking. After they are diagnosed with excessive stress, they are ready to stop working 12 hours a day and get eight hours of sleep each night. After a divorce, they decide to seek counseling. After a bankruptcy, they are willing to do a business plan. After they lose their job, they are willing to report to work on time. After they lose all their money playing the lottery or horses, they are now willing to return the tithes and offerings. Failure after failure, they are willing to read the Word of God, study and meditate to get inspired on how to become successful.

The reason I understand "after people" so well is because I used to be one of them! Thank God for His grace. Today, I am a passionate member of the "before" people.

There is nothing wrong with practicing prevention.

I have been given the opportunity to live an abundant life by embracing a thought development lifestyle. You are your thoughts and your thoughts are your power, the power God has given you. There is only one power and that is the power of God.

> *Behold, I give you the authority to trample on serpents and scorpions, and over all the power of the enemy, and nothing shall by any means hurt you.*
> (Luke 10:19)

Many people I know are preoccupied with anxiety, worry, and a sin consciousness. These people are also preoccupied with other people's sin, and love to send rich and wealthy people to hell. These preoccupations are ungodly and unhealthy, and contribute to fostering bad thoughts or a thought reactionary lifestyle.

May I state the obvious? It is very difficult for anyone to stay healthy and whole while criticizing and cursing people who are prosperous, rich or wealthy. Fewer people would need healing crusades and doctors if they would change

31

their thought stimuli from a *thought reactionary lifestyle* to a thought development lifestyle.

I used to place blame on the devil for my crazy thoughts. After placing the blame on the devil, I still had the same thought problems. I used to blame God for all of my problems (many people do the same thing) until I took responsibility for my own thoughts. When I started obeying Romans 12:1-2 my life began to change.

I beseech you therefore, brethren, by the mercies of God, that ye present your bodies a living sacrifice, holy, acceptable unto God, which is your reasonable service. And be not conformed to this world: but be ye transformed by the renewing of your mind, that ye may prove what is that good, and acceptable, and perfect, will of God.

(Romans 12:1-2)

Those words made me realize that God has given me the power over my own thought life. I realized that I had a free will to choose, to think any way I desired, and that I must take the responsibility for the consequences of my thinking and thoughts...whether good or bad.

Someone once said (I do not remember who):

• A person's confession or response is the result of their belief.
• A person's belief is the result of their thoughts.
• A person's thoughts are the result of their knowledge
• A person's knowledge is a result of their source.

There are four major sources of power, but only one true power: God.

Satan as a source is a defeated power, the world as a source is trying to substitute God's real power, but it is a fabricated world power, and man is a source of power, but does not realize that God is the only true source of all power. The source you use for your power will determine your thoughts.

The Seven Types of Thought

In 2002, Brother Randy Shankle, my spiritual father, brought an excellent teaching on thoughts and thinking. Listed below are several types of thinking that I know will bless you. They are the types of thinking we need to employ to be like the ant in Proverbs 6:6-8:

Go to the ant, thou sluggard; consider her ways, and be wise: Which having no guide, overseer, or ruler, Provideth her meat in the summer, and gathereth her food in the harvest.

1. Initiative thinking...getting things ready.
2. Motivational thinking...getting things going.
3. Solutional thinking...getting things solved.
4. Incentive thinking...getting things done.
5. Controlled thinking...getting things under control.
6. Focused thinking...getting things together.
7. Renewed thinking...getting things right.

The Model for Change: Change Your Thoughts

Mental hospitals are full of people whose thoughts are not right.

Be renewed in the spirit of your mind. Be renewed in the spirit of your thoughts which results in a fresh mental and spiritual attitude.
                                    (Ephesians 4:23 Amplified Version.)

The jails and prisons are overcrowded with people with wrong thinking. Many politicians and government officials serve in office with bad thoughts.

There can be no real change with people in mental hospitals, prisons, corporations, churches, universities and colleges until you help change the thoughts of these people.

In Atlanta, Georgia, I attended Samuel Dewitt Proctor's Pastors' Conference in 2004, where the term "transformative paradigm" was used. I define this new "transformative paradigm" as "a revolution of thought change." There cannot be any significant change in people's lives until pastors, apostles, corporation presidents, and world leaders work to help people change their thoughts. Transformative movements are fine, but without a thought change, the movement will die.

All new innovations, discoveries, and advancements in all spheres of life come from people who are renewing their minds or thought lives.

The crime problem in the world is due to bad thoughts. Racism is a result of wrong thinking about people. When racism is practiced, it hurts the promoter of racism more than the victim of it. The perpetrators of racism usually experience both mental and physical problems as a result of this hatred of others.

In America, money alone does not solve people's problems. America has wasted trillions of dollars to wipe out poverty, and yet millions of people still live in poverty. There must be a thought change in America.

Stop Blaming the Devil! Stop Sinning!

Now is the day to "recover" yourself from the captivity and the snares of the devil. He has a plan and a trap for you, but you do not need to enter into his trap. Stay in the Spirit and under the anointing of God and you will not get trapped. I've heard some say, "Oh, that woman. I went to bed with her. I got trapped." Well, no, you wanted to be trapped! Your thoughts trap you.

The flow of money into your life is *not* being held up by the devil, nor by the economy, nor by the welfare system, nor by affirmative action, nor by quotas, nor by hand outs, nor by government grants, nor by the white man, nor by the black man nor the green man. You are the one who has caused the flow to stop! In Alcoholics Anonymous, they tell you, "First, you must identify your problem, then accept responsibility for your problem."

Whatever condition you are in today, you did it to yourself unless you are living in an oppressive, military-controlled country, a country that constantly oppresses its people!

The Anointing–the Source of Your Supply

> *But my God shall supply all your need according to his riches in glory by Christ Jesus.*
>
> (Philippians 4:19)

God can supply all you need to erase that which is genetic, that which has been twisted and turned in your life. God can, through you, turn your life around. It makes no difference how or where you were born. I was reared in foster homes, but so what? Now it is our challenge to birth a life where our faith is toward God.

Once you recognize *you* have the problem of opposing yourself, then *you* must decide to do something about. You must decide you are not going to be the one who works all of your days so that at retirement you receive a watch. In the typical "wage-earner mentality," people just go from transition to transition. Statistics say that most retirees die three to five years after retirement. Instead, I believe God wants His people to view retirement as a time to fire-up for God, the opportunity to find greater work to do in the Kingdom of God. He has more for you as you tap into His anointing to release your money and your wealth. It is time for "refirement" not retirement.

Trust God. He has a better future for you. Listen to the Holy Ghost. Let Him help you to examine yourself, and then turn your faith toward God.

> *For I know that this will turn out for my salvation through your prayer and the supply of the Spirit of Jesus Christ.*
>
> (Philippians 1:19)

35

In the above Scripture, the word "supply" comes from "epichoregia" which means, "it is the contribution" of the Holy Spirit to bring about your release, anointing your life for money, materials, wealth or whatever the Lord wants to pour into your life.

Something is going to break loose that is already in you, called "the anointing of Christ." You already have it in residence. This book will help you get it out of you so you can be successful in the things of God...in your finances, in your material needs, and in your walk toward divine health. The next chapter will help you refocus your view of money so you can obtain the anointing.

The work of the Spirit is going to activate your money to furnish your finances.

A Special Money Supply

The word "supply" in this passage also means "minister." God wants to "minister" to furnish you finances. The work of the Holy Spirit is to activate your money through the *special money supply* in the anointing. You must get out of yourself and get in faith toward God so you can receive. Your money is coming not because of your job or business, but because of the anointings. And your renewed thoughts.

"Epichoregia" means "to furnish." The work of the Spirit will activate a special money supply in the anointing of Christ in your life.

"How do I get all this money?"

Through a special money supply anointing on your life. God will furnish finances through you. Your money is going to flow in the realm of the Spirit as you stop sowing in the flesh. Sowing in the flesh is a deception to keep your eyes blind so you cannot receive the anointing in the realm of the spirit.

"My God shall supply all of my needs" means that He is going to fill your financial requests as you release a financial seed to the apostolic work of God. Put this next statement deep in your new mind and lock it there forever:

"There is a spiritual supply for every need through the work of the anointing of the pneuma, the Spirit."

Your anointing is already inside of you, trying to get out, but it can't because you have not learned how to maximize the anointings within you. God is in you trying to get out in the earth. God wants to manifest Himself through you in the earth through His anointings.

How many of you have boiled some greens until the kettle starts shaking? It looks like those greens want to get out, but they can't get out until you take the lid off.

The anointing is already inside of you, boiling away, wanting to get out, to flow in you, through you and out of you so you can impact and bless others. But like the greens boiling in the kettle, it can't escape.

Self (your non-spiritual lid) is holding in your anointing.

The Purpose of the Money Anointing

There is a spiritual supply for every need through the work of the anointing of the Holy Spirit. *The purpose* of your supply is to aide or contribute, to add money, finances, materials, wealth, wisdom, and abundance...through you so God can use you to help establish His covenant in the earth.

And thou say in thine heart, My power and the might of mine hand hath gotten me this wealth. But thou shalt remember the LORD thy God: for it is He that giveth thee power to get wealth, that he may establish his covenant which he sware unto thy fathers (Abraham), as it is this day.

(Deuteronomy 8:17-18)

37

Do you see it? You and I are the seed of Abraham, and the purpose of our supply is so God can establish His covenant in the city where we live! The covenant He made with Abraham was good then, it is good for 2004, and it will be good for 2040!

> *And if ye be Christ's, then ye are Abraham's seed, and heirs according to the promise."*
>
> (Galatians 3:29)

So, the purpose of your supply is to establish His Kingdom covenant in the earth, and to receive the heritage of Abraham in your life today. The Old Testament word for "anointing" was "shemen," as in "the anointing" (shemen) shall destroy the yoke (Isaiah 10:27). You have an anointing from the Old Testament, and that anointing is still real today! You are an heir to what God promised Abraham because you are Abraham's seed.

The power is in your hands to get riches. God has highly anointed your hands, and it does not matter if you are skilled or unskilled. Someone said that you are the generational wealth of God.

The anointing of God is there for you to receive wealth.

When that anointing is released through your God-consciousness, money will flow through you, to help establish God's Kingdom on earth or support His Apostolic work. The Apostolic work is the work of Jesus as Chief Apostle by expanding it throughout the earth.

In the following chapters I will share with you the revelations you need to help you unlock God's miraculous, life-transforming money anointing in your life!

Purpose Versus Divine Destiny

Know your purpose in life.

Your purpose must bring you into your destiny; if it doesn't, you have the wrong purpose. Purpose and destiny are interconnecting truths that tie into everything you do, even releasing of the money anointing upon your life.

In this section, I want to honor Dr. Mark Hanby for helping me to understand purpose and destiny from a greater dimension. I even see money in a different light as a result of understanding purpose, destiny and the tabernacle of Moses in greater depth. I believe this book, *Releasing the Money Anointing*, is my destiny as well as yours.

I was recently in Santa Rosa Beach, Florida (January 2004), where I met (I believe "divinely met") Dr. Mark Hanby at a Gold's Gym. I had never met this man before. But, as a result of this on-the-spot, divine connection, I immediately was awakened to destiny on a greater dimension than I had ever known before.

Soon after that, we met again, spending time together (along with Alex McEntire, another apostle who was with me from Cincinnati). I was amazed that this man, who did not know me, would spend some time with me; Dr. Hanby knows and meets many important people from all over the world. He is a spiritual father to many great men and women throughout our nation. Dr. Hanby also recognized that this was a *divine* connection; that's why he moved his schedule around to meet with us.

I am totally convinced that you can receive spiritual, apostolic impartations from others in a moment, in the twinkling of an eye—when destiny is at hand. That is what happened to me that day on the beach with Dr. Hanby as he shared revelations on the three dimensions of grace.

On the beach where Dr. Hanby spends time with the Lord, he imparted to us like Jesus did to the disciples. He picked up a stick and began drawing in the sand the tabernacle of Moses. (What a great day to receive impartation from such a Godly man!) He opened up a revelation on the tabernacle of Moses in such a way that it brought us into instant destiny at a greater level of grace.

Dr. Hanby used the tabernacle of Moses to share both natural and spiritual things with us.

> *However, the spiritual is not first, but the natural, and afterward the spiritual.*
>
> (I Corinthians 15:46)

Dr. Hanby used the backdrop of John on the Isle of Patmos.

> *I, John, both your brother and companion in the tribulation and kingdom and patience of Jesus Christ, was on the island that is called Patmos for the word of God and for the testimony of Jesus Christ. I was in the Spirit on the Lord's Day, and I heard behind me a loud voice, as of a trumpet.*
>
> (Revelation 1:9-10)

For about two hours, Dr. Hanby shared with us how a thousand years is as a day to the Lord, and demonstrated this in the sand, drawing a 7,000- year-span of history, and demonstrating how it connected to the seven days of Creation, the tabernacle of Moses, and John's experience on the Isle of Patmos. Dr. Hanby talked about how the work was finished from the very foundations of the world.

> *For we who have believed do enter that rest, as He has said: "So I swore in My wrath, They shall not enter My rest," although the works were finished from the foundation of the world.*
>
> (Hebrews 4:3)

> *But, beloved, do not forget this one thing, that with the Lord one day is as a thousand years, and a thousand years as one day.*
>
> (II Peter 3:8)

> *For He has spoken in a certain place of the seventh day in this way: "And God rested on the seventh day from all His works;" and again in this place: "They shall not enter My rest." Since therefore it remains*

40

*that some must enter it, and those to whom it was
first preached did not enter because of disobedience,
again He designates a certain day, saying in David,
"Today," after such a long time, as it has been said:
"Today, if you will hear His voice, do not harden your
hearts." For if Joshua had given them rest, then He
would not afterward have spoken of another day.
There remains therefore a rest for the people of God.
For he who has entered His rest has himself also
ceased from his works as God did from His. Let us
therefore be diligent to enter that rest, lest anyone fall
according to the same example of disobedience.*

(Hebrews 4:4-11)

Dr. Hanby told us that we have entered the seventh
millennium of destiny. He disclosed to us how, in the
tabernacle of Moses, the outer court was the fifth day, or five
thousand years; the Holy place was the sixth day, or six
thousand years; the most Holy Place was the seventh day, or
seven thousand years. He used the tabernacle to show us the
three dimensions of grace in the tabernacle, sharing how this
teaching brings us into greater dimensions of grace in God.
(If you want to hear the entire teaching on this subject, go to
Dr. Mark Hanby's Website, at www.Hanby.org, and purchase
the video, "The Voice Behind Me.")

As Dr. Hanby taught on this beautiful Florida beach, he
tied the teaching to purpose and destiny, giving me a
greater revelation on the purpose of money versus releasing
the money anointing—which is our destiny.

According to *Roget's II–The New Thesaurus Third
Edition*, "purpose" is "what one intends to do or achieve.
Purpose is the proper activity of a person or thing, function,
job, role and task." Roget's further states that, "to be
purposeless is to be without aim, intent or aimless." I
believe that Myles Monroe stated it best when he said,
"When you don't understand the purpose of a thing, you will
abuse it."

Roget's II–the New Thesaurus defines "destiny" as "that which is inevitable." Destiny is predestation, and predestation is destiny. Destiny is eternity. You can enjoy eternal life now if you understand how purpose and destiny work and connect together.

> *Having predestinated us unto the adoption of children by Jesus Christ to himself, according to the good pleasure of his will.*
>
> (Ephesians 1:5)

We were created before the foundation of the world. We are already flowing in our destiny, but most people do not realize this truth. That is why purpose needs to bring you into your destiny.

> *Just as He chose us in Him before the foundation of the world, that we should be holy and without blame before Him in love,*
>
> (Ephesians 1:4)

Rule and Reign Now!

Purpose should unlock your eternity and bring you into the dimensions of the anointings and presence of a loving God (which is destiny), so you can rule and reign right now.

Your purpose must take you into your destiny.

Everything you do must either help bring you into your destiny or help you fulfill your destiny.

> *And we know that all things work together for good to them that love God, to them who are the called according to his purpose.*
>
> (Romans 8:28)

Purpose should link or connect you to destiny. If your purpose is not getting you into your destiny, you are living in a circle and going nowhere. We need the counsel of skillful and knowledgeable people like Dr. Hanby to help us develop good and Godly purpose with a view towards destiny.

Reading the Bible is *purpose*, but *living* the Bible is *destiny*! When we live the Bible, our lives become a living epistle in the earth and heaven.

> *You are our epistle written in our hearts, known and read by all men;*
>
> (II Corinthians 3:2)

> *Every purpose is established by counsel: and with good advice make war.*
>
> (Proverbs 20:18)

Purpose is *ministry to each other*. However, destiny is *ministry* to *the people in the world*. We must begin to reach out and love all people, demonstrating our love to the world. That is destiny!

Purpose is *trying*, while destiny is *being*.

Purpose does not reproduce, while destiny reproduces.

The key to the Kingdom is purpose, while using the keys is destiny. You must use your keys to come into your greater dimension of the Kingdom of grace. Here are some examples of what I mean.

It is a good purpose to get married, but if that person does not link you to your destiny, you will just have a marriage of purpose.

It is excellent to join a church, but if that church does not connect you to your destiny, you will never come into the Kingdom of God in a greater dimension of grace.

It may be fine to own a business that creates millions of dollars, however, if your business, employment or money does not connect you to, or further your destiny, then all you have is money with a wrong purpose.

And I will give unto thee the keys of the kingdom of heaven: and whatsoever thou shalt bind on earth shall be bound in heaven: and whatsoever thou shalt loose on earth shall be loosed in heaven.

(Matthew 16:19)

Your purpose will not get you into your destiny, and without your destiny, you are living life in a circle!

Purpose is *hearing*, while destiny is *doing*.

"Kingdom Now" Thinking

If you don't renew your mind or change your thoughts, you will not come into your destiny.

I beseech you therefore, brethren, by the mercies of God, that ye present your bodies a living sacrifice, holy, acceptable unto God, which is your reasonable service. And be not conformed to this world: but be ye transformed by the renewing of your mind, that ye may prove what is that good, and acceptable, and perfect, will of God.

(Romans 12:1-2)

You are really not living the abundant life until you step into your destiny. Don't be limited by wrong purpose. Destiny is much bigger than your local church, your state, America, the nations and even the universe.

Destiny is living in the realm of the third heaven, while also living on earth.

Destiny is a lifestyle. Destiny is reproduction, creation, and generation. Destiny says "We have the Kingdom of God now!" Destiny is ascension with Christ now. Destiny states, "We have heaven on earth now." Destiny is ruling and reigning now!

When you understand and live in your destiny, time is not as important. Destiny is eternal. Destiny is a greater dimension of God.

While we look not at the things which are seen, but at the things which are not seen: for the things which are seen are temporal; but the things which are not seen are eternal.

(II Corinthians 4:18)

This is your time to experience the wealth, abundance, and grace of God on a new level–now! Yes, destiny is the Kingdom of God, and everyone is welcome to join. If you don't fulfill your destiny, you will die in your purpose.

On the other hand, for those who are fulfilling their destiny, and die a physical death, be assured that you will live on in eternity, knowing that nothing changes but your physical body.

For we know that if our earthly house of this tabernacle were dissolved, we have a building of God, an house not made with hands, eternal in the heavens.

(II Corinthians 5:1)

Destiny is reproduction of your sonship in the earth. If you don't reproduce yourself in other people, you are not fulfilling destiny! You are only making love with your purpose. In other words, destiny is making disciples!

Go then and make disciples of all the nations, baptizing them into the name of the Father and of the Son and of the Holy Spirit,
(Matthew 28:19, The Amplified Bible)

Destiny is "the third dimension of grace" where the throne of God dwells and occupies. Everything we do should get us to our destiny. Don't get comfortable with your purpose and miss your destiny. Destiny is your eternal purpose.

According to the eternal purpose which he purposed in Christ Jesus our Lord:

(Ephesians 3:11)

The Apostolic Revolution

The new, apostolic revolution that is taking place in the earth is being built on the perfect love of God to take the fear out of the hearts of the people. God loves you so much and He wants you to come into your destiny. And, we have a new brand of love—apostles in the earth—to help you with these divine connections and impartations (yes, that is a part of my calling).

The Lord has pulled every wall down in every aspect and sphere of society so that you can be free. The new apostles and prophets will help activate and release the manifestation of the sons and daughters throughout the earth into their destiny. As this release evolves, the world will be so fascinated with this new apostolic revolution that it will include them (even though the Church has let them down in the past).

Life, liberty and the pursuit of joy is the destiny you deserve.

The apostolic revolution of destiny is spreading in the workplace and marketplace in an unprecedented way. God has sent a final message, especially to the Church and to some leaders, which states: "Let my people go so that they can come into their destiny."

The Lord says, "The spirit of religion, control and manipulation has been broken. Go forth, My sons and daughters, without fear, into your apostolic destiny."

The Church has isolated herself from the people in the world. The church is the purpose, but the Kingdom of God is the destiny. You cannot afford to get stuck in the corporate church as we know it. Dr. Hanby calls the present church structure the second dimension. We need to come into the third dimension of destiny. The Church comes out of the Kingdom, and is also the third dimension of grace. If the Church cannot bring people into their destiny, then it will remain powerless to change the world.

It will remain powerless to enjoy the earth with peace and righteousness in the Holy Spirit.

Eternal Destiny

When you understand and come into your destiny, you will never again worry about the issue of mortality.

Now unto the King eternal, immortal, invisible, the only wise God, be honour and glory for ever and ever. Amen.

(I Timothy 1:17)

Being born again, not of corruptible seed, but of incorruptible, by the word of God, which liveth and abideth for ever.

(I Peter 1:23)

And every man that striveth for the mastery is temperate in all things. Now they do it to obtain a corruptible crown; but we an incorruptible.

(I Corinthians 9:25)

For to me to live is Christ, and to die is gain. But if I live in the flesh, this is the fruit of my labour: yet what I shall choose I want not. For I am in a strait betwixt two, having a desire to depart, and to be with Christ; which is far better:

(Philippians 1:21-23)

Destiny is immortality and eternity.

Destiny is the heavenly place, the third dimension of grace.

And hath raised us up together, and made us sit together in heavenly places in Christ Jesus: That in the ages to come he might shew the exceeding riches of his grace in his kindness toward us through Christ Jesus.

(Ephesians 2:6-7)

Enjoy the earth in the physical realm because you have the confidence and assurance that you are already seated in heavenly place. Yes, you will one day die a physical death, but you shall live forever! This is a great and spiritual paradox—living and dying at the same time. Yes, you are seated over death, the devil, hell, and the lake of fire.

And whosoever liveth and believeth in me shall never die. Believest thou this?

(John 11:26)

For our conversation is in heaven; from whence also we look for the Saviour, the Lord Jesus Christ: Who shall change our vile body, that it may be fashioned like unto his glorious body, according to the working whereby he is able even to subdue all things unto himself.

(Philippians 3:20-21)

When you come into your destiny, you will conquer sin, death, and hell because you will be above it, seated in heavenly places. When you come into your destiny, you can get caught up now, and at the same time, enjoy the earth.

The earth is the LORD'S, and the fullness thereof; the world, and they that dwell therein.

(Psalm 24:1)

Jesus said to the thief in Luke 23:43, *"This day you shall be with me in Paradise."* Jesus knew you could enjoy the earth while, at the same time, live in a spiritual paradise or eternal bliss.

Apostles are popping up all over the earth like Jim Becton, Earl Paulk, Mark Hanby, Randy Shankle, Chuck Pierce, Peter Wagner and others to help move people from purpose to destiny. To understand how that is working, you need only to remember the brief encounter Alex and I had with Dr. Hanby, and how that so dramatically impacted us, giving us a quick revelation of the Spirit (especially through his message on, " The Voice Behind Me"). *"Blessed are they which hunger and thirst after righteousness* (or destiny) *for they shall be filled with it."* (Matthew 5:6)

Destiny People and Money

Now that you have a deeper understanding of purpose and destiny, let us consider the purpose and the destiny of money.

The purpose of money is to help bring you into your destiny.

The possession of money, just for the sake of having money, will remain as a wrong purpose which can lead to greed and corruption. Until you circulate money–to connect and link people to their destiny–you will not have achieved very much.

Money is to be used to bless others!

Blessing mankind is the destiny. Therefore, money, abundance, surplus, and prosperity is for destiny people.

When money is just purpose, then destiny will not be achieved. Once you understand destiny, you will see money in a totally different perspective.

Destiny people...

- Handle money without shame and guilt.
- Know how to use and circulate money.
- Release the money anointing to address the financial need or challenges for self and others.
- Produce and reproduce surplus, creating revenue streams for others.
- Understand money on the highest spiritual level.
- Know that spiritual blessings are given to them now, such as the anointing, glory and presence of God, divine health, wealth and prosperity. Remember you are the wealth of God in the earth.

- Become money masters, and are not servants of money!

Paul, an apostle of Jesus Christ by the will of God, to the saints which are at Ephesus, and to the faithful in Christ Jesus: Grace be to you, and peace, from God our Father, and from the Lord Jesus Christ. Blessed be the God and Father of our Lord Jesus Christ, who hath blessed us with all spiritual blessings in heavenly places in Christ: According as He hath chosen us in Him before the foundation of the world, that we should be holy and without blame before Him in love: Having predestinated us unto the adoption of children by Jesus Christ to Himself, according to the good pleasure of His will.

(Ephesians 1:1-5)

In whom also we have obtained an inheritance, being predestinated according to the purpose of him who worketh all things after the counsel of his own will.

(Ephesians 1:11)

The Three Dimensions of Money

There are three types or dimensions of money, and when I write about money, I am talking about the highest level.

The Bible expresses itself in sets of three. "The number 'three' means 'the number of the Godhead, the number of divine completeness, the perfect testimony.'" (Kevin J. Conner 's book, *The Symbols and Types*, 1980.) These various dimensions of three can be seen in twenty-two major biblical areas:

1. Thirty, Sixty and Hundredfold.
2. The Blade, The Ear and the Full Corn.
3. Revelation, Transformation and Manifestation.
4. First Heaven, Second Heaven and Third Heaven.
5. Spirit, Soul and Body.
6. Father, Son and Holy Spirit.

7. Outer Court, Holy Place and Most Holy Place.
8. Passover, Pentecost and Tabernacles.
9. Kingly, Priestly, and Prophetic Anointing.
10. Spiritual, Domestic and Civil Authority.
11. Jesus raised on the Third Day.
12. Death, Burial and Resurrection.
13. Paul and John Visited the Third Heaven.
14. Apostles, Prophets and Teachers.
15. On the East Three Gates, on the North Three Gates, On the South Three Gates, On the West Three Gates.
16. The Spirit, the Water and the Blood.
17. Husband, Wife and Children
18. Father, Mother and Children
19. Faith, Hope and Love
20. The Way, the Truth and Life
21. Peter, James and John
22. First, second and third dimensions of grace.

Coming into the third dimension is living in the Spirit, the Holy Place, the tabernacle, the hundredfold blessing, in the Third Heaven. Living in the third dimension is the manifestation, authority and anointing, and walking in the fullness and stature of Christ, the Anointed, experiencing His Anointing in every sphere of the earth.

There are also three dimensions of money: **material money**, **mind money** and **spiritual money**.

First, let us look at the two dimensions of material money.

1. Material Money

A. Dimension One: Promotes Materialism and Consumerism

The lowest level of money is when money is used to promote materialism and consumerism. It is obtaining money just for the sake of money. Greed comes from being a materialist. Seeking money to have and to hold can lead to doing corrupt things to generate money. One can be a materialist without having any money–because money can be a bad thought. Materialism is a pursuit of the heart to have and possess money for the sake of it. Material money is a type and shadow of the outer court of the tabernacle of Moses. Material money is outer court money. Obtaining money only on the material level will lead to greed if your mind is not transformed at the Most Holy Place.

B. Dimension Two: Manifested Money

"Soma" is the Greek word for "body," and it denotes the physical realm. "Soma" is the physical money we circulate and use when money is put into our hands. "Soma" is "manifested money" to be wonderfully used to bless people. Jesus used a parable to demonstrate the proper use of money in Luke 19:13:

> *So he called ten of his servants and gave them ten minas. Put this money to work; he said until I come back.*
>
> (NIV)

> *So he called ten of his servants, delivered to them ten minas, and said to them, do business till I come.*
> (NKJV)

2. Mind Money

A. Dimension One: Psyche or Soul Money

The word "psyche" means "soul" in the Greek. It represents your mind, emotions, will, intellect, thoughts and senses. Psyche money is usually based on meeting some financial need or request.

Many people feel better when they have money, and feel badly when they don't. Emotional money can play games with your emotions until you constantly renew your mind with the Word of God so that you will be able to control your emotions—whether you have money or not! You must manage your emotions so money and other things won't affect your emotions.

If your mind is properly renewed daily, you will master money and money will not master you! If you think proper thoughts about money, money will not control you but will serve you. You must be transformed by the renewing of your psyche (mind).

You must control your mind by programming it with the Word of God. The soul is a quiet listener and receives impressions from what is spoken. The mind causes you to act on these messages. If you constantly are saying negative and crazy things during your self-talk, this silent listener of the soul will cause you to act on these negative thoughts. That is why you need to continually be transformed by the renewal of your mind (instead of the removal of your mind).

B.   Dimension Two: Transformative Money

The Psyche Realm is the soul or mind level (some call this the "psychic level" of money). For you to handle money at the material or spiritual level, you need to renew your mind at the mind level.

Mind money is inner court money. The Most Holy Place is when your mind is transformed with the Word of God. When the mind is transformed, you use money responsibly and appropriately to bless others (without a wrong motivation or greed) because your mind is right.

The anointed mind is the result of your spiritual awareness about who you are in God. It is this spiritual dimension that aides in the transformation of your mind to a renewed one.

If you don't change your thought life, there will be no real change in your mind, physical body or decisions. As you renew your mind in the Word of God, you will begin to think right about material money.

Learning to put your mind and body at rest is a key so that the renewing of the mind process can be effective. There are 10 practical principles of healthy living recommended by "Trivita—The Healthy Living Company" in Scottsdale, Arizona.

Ten Practical Principles for Healthy Living

1. Breathe deeply.
2. Drink water.
3. Sleep peacefully.
4. Eat nutritiously.
5. Enjoy activity.
6. Give and receive.
7. Be forgiving.
8. Practice gratitude.
9. Develop acceptance.
10. Develop a relationship with God.

3. Spiritual Money

A. Dimension One: Spirit Money

There are billions of people on the earth who don't believe that they are worthy, or good enough, to have money because someone told them, "Money is evil and it will corrupt them." It constantly amazes me that these same people have not yet found a way to live on this earth without this so called "evil money." I have never seen any "evil money," but I have met many evil people with money.

Someone once said, "Money is spiritual because it takes on the spirit of the person who possesses it." An evil spirit equals evil money, a Godly spirit equals Godly money. Dr. Paula A. Price in her book, *Money Is a Spirit*, states: "The transformation starts with accepting that money is a spirit." Spiritual money is the Most Holy Place money. It is the money that you obtain in the realm of the Holy Spirit. It is money that you have in the spirit before it is manifested in the natural. When the mind is transformed, spiritual money becomes a reality for manifestation. She elaborates, "I repeat it to establish its pulsing truth in you to break every chain and shackle of debt, lack and poverty by getting you to change your present money thinking and thought self-talk."

The spiritual money dimension is the highest level of money! This level is the focus of *Releasing the Money Anointing*. Spiritual money is the foundation of my entire book. Once you understand the spiritual levels of the money anointing, you can use the money anointing to walk in character, wealth, abundance, prosperity, and divine health.

Just as there is a preaching anointing, a teaching anointing, and a healing anointing, there is also a money anointing. How you ultimately use your money in the earth is determined by how well you understand the anointing. Three basic principles dominate that understanding:

Principle One: Money should be used to be a blessing to you and your family.

Principle Two: Money should be used to be a blessing to others.

Principle Three: Money should be used to finance the apostolic work of God in the earth such as: television, radio, Web sites, satellites, planting of new apostolic works, international and global apostolic works. This new money should also be used for apostolic encampments, research, technology, discovery of new healing technology and advancement, scientific discoveries, and initiatives to eradicate heart disease, cancer and strokes.

If you operate from a spiritual perspective, you can use, circulate, and enjoy money without being corrupt, or without any fear of evil coming to you because you possess money.

    B.   Dimension Two: <u>Pneuma–Revelation Money</u>

The "Pneuma" realm is the highest spiritual level of money. It is receiving money in the unseen realm *before* you have material money. The "seeing money" is money you see before it materializes physically, and it is the greatest money you can ever have or possess. This is money before it touches your physical hand.

Releasing the money anointing starts at this level.

"Pneuma" is the Greek word for "spirit." The Pneuma level is where you experience money in the unseen realm of the spirit. As you are transformed in your mind or psyche, you will start realizing money on the material or manifested level where you can touch it and feel it.

The focus of *Releasing the Money Anointing* is the spiritual dimension of money where you meet God face-to-face as your source. Mankind is your channel to bless you financially, but God is the source of your money, your healing, your deliverance, and your divine health. This level of money is not based upon the amount of money a person has accumulated, *but the amount of anointing a person possesses*.

This kind of money has nothing to do with a personal net worth statement! The anointing determines how much peace, joy, divine health, and mind health you will have in handling your money release.

A person, at this Pneuma level, may not necessarily have millions or billions of dollars in the bank, but they do have *favor, good ideas, wisdom and witty inventions* with a view towards creating money.

Money at the spiritual dimension is ultimately to be used as a blessing to others. Giving your anointing, life, and money away is part of the spiritual dimension release process where you recognize that you are indeed the wealth of God.

When you circulate money to others, it always comes back to you.

Are You Wealthy?

There are four major indicators that determine if you are wealthy. The first three must be in divine order in your life. Financial health is only beneficial to the degree that the first three indicators are in place.

The first three divine priorities are based on III John 3:

Beloved, I wish above all things that thou mayest __prosper__ and be in __health__, even as thy __soul__ prospers.

Indicator One: Spiritual Health

Having a right and proper relationship with God and others is vital. Love the Lord with all of your heart and soul, and love your neighbor as yourself. Learn to walk in the anointing, the glory and presence of God, both in heavenly places and on earth. Know that God is really your source for everything.

Indicator Two: Physical Health

You need to have a physical body that is constantly being healed by your walk in divine health, using the principals of proper nutrition, diet, exercise, and sleep to maintain a healthy body. It is your right to have divine health.

Indicator Three: Mind Health

It is important to have your mind renewed in the Word of God, moment-by-moment, as well as by reading inspiring books. Maintain a stable, sound, and sober mind. Be alert and make rational, clear decisions in order to maintain a healthy mind and body.

The transformation of your mind on a daily basis must be a priority. It is your right to have a sound mind! You need to feed on the Word of God as well as the proceeding voice of God. You must live by every word that proceeds out of the mouth of God.

It is written, "Man shall not live by bread alone, but by every word that proceeds from the mouth of God."
(Matthew 4:4)

Indicator Four: Financial Success

Have a financial plan for your life; determine the amount of surplus money you will need to fulfill your destiny goals on earth. Generate and circulate money to be a blessing to you, your family and the world...it is your right.

Once people understand that they have been made after the image and likeness of God, they then can experience the invasion of God in every aspect of their life. We were created before the foundation of the world at the highest spiritual level so we can obtain everything we need in this realm of the spirit, such as health, healing, money and love.

The majority of people who are successful financially utilize the Biblical laws and principles listed here to expand their financial base:

1. Giving and receiving.
2. Sowing and reaping.
3. Seed-time and harvest.
4. Tithes and Offering.
5. Investing, returning, stocks, bonds and real estate.
6. Savings.
7. Planting and watering.
8. Uncommon seed sowing and first fruit offerings.
9. The green principle: become accustomed to the color of money (in other words, they become comfortable with green money).

The Violation of Spiritual Laws
Creates Money Problems

Many people do not live an abundant life because they lack an understanding, or violate spiritual laws. They reject the releasing of the money anointing, the healing anointing, the preaching anointing, the glory and presence of God, because they hold these seven false beliefs.

Seven False Beliefs that Hinder the Anointing

1.   Refusing to accept that God created all things, first in the spiritual and then in the natural—that is God's order of things.

Howbeit that was not first which is spiritual, but that which is natural; and afterward that which is spiritual.

(I Cor. 15:46)

2.   Refusing to accept the truth that they were created before the foundation of the earth.

According as He hath chosen us in Him before the foundation of the world, that we should be holy and without blame before Him in love:

(Ephesians 1:4)

3.   Refusing to accept the truth that they came from God, and were created in His image and likeness. Ninety-nine percent of mankind believes that, "I came from Adam, and I am just a sinner saved by grace. That's the way it is going to be the rest of my life." These people fail to understand that Christ, the second Adam, came to earth to reconcile them back to their image and likeness of God! Confess the Lordship of Christ and that will take care of the destruction of the sin consciousness you have been taught.

That if thou shalt confess with thy mouth the Lord Jesus, and shalt believe in thine heart that God hath raised him from the dead, thou shalt be saved. For with the heart man believeth unto righteousness; and with the mouth confession is made unto salvation,

(Romans 10:9-10)

And God said, Let us make man in our image, after our likeness: and let them have dominion over the fish of the sea, and over the fowl of the air, and over the cattle, and over all the earth, and over every creeping thing that creepeth upon the earth.

(Genesis 1:26)

4.   Refusing to accept a righteousness conscious-ness, instead choosing to live in a sin-consciousness and a self-consciousness which leads to a problem-life instead of a destiny-driven life. According to Dr. Creflo A. Dollar, Jr., in his book, *The Image of Righteousness*, "The word 'justified' means declared righteousness.' In other words, we are righteous for no other reason than the fact that God has declared us righteous."

And God said, Let us make man in our image, after our likeness: and let them have dominion over the fish of the sea, and over the fowl of the air, and over the cattle, and over all the earth, and over every creeping thing that creepeth upon the earth.

(Romans 1:17)

5.   Denying and disregarding the unseen or invisible realm of the spirit of God. A great majority of mankind believe that all things are only natural or material. Many people, including the majority of the Church, reject their deity and instead only embrace their humanity, not seeing themselves as spirit beings with delegated power from God.

Humanity, without the spirit dominating or ruling, is no more than an animal or a beast out of control.

We are both natural and divine! Your divine must

rule over your natural. God in us is both human and divine. Our body and soul must be ruled by our spirit. If not, our destiny is a miserable life on earth.

While we look not at the things which are seen, but at the things which are not seen: for the things which are seen are temporal; but the things which are not seen are eternal.

(II Cor. 4:18)

6.   Refusing to have faith toward God and practice the laws of faith. Refusal to accept the basic foundation stones of God.

For unto us was the gospel preached, as well as unto them: but the word preached did not profit them, not being mixed with faith in them that heard it.

(Hebrews 4:2)

Therefore leaving the principles of the doctrine of Christ, let us go on unto perfection; not laying again the foundation of repentance from dead works, and of faith toward God, Of the doctrine of baptisms, and of laying on of hands, and of resurrection of the dead, and of eternal judgment. And this will we do, if God permit.

(Hebrews 6:1-3)

7.   Accepting a philosophy of limitation, lack and want, believing that God wants them to suffer, that somehow God wants to punish them and send them to hell if they are not good. They silently believe that God is working against them. God is not working for you, He's working through you.

Thank God for the late Kenneth E. Hagin! In 1972, I was introduced to his teachings, and especially appreciate his great teachings on faith contained in *Redeemed From Poverty, Sickness and Spiritual Death.* Brother Hagin's teachings helped me as a believer; I could not have completed this book without a thorough understanding of how I was redeemed by Jesus Christ and freed from poverty, sickness, and spiritual death.

For I know the thoughts that I think toward you, saith the LORD, thoughts of peace, and not of evil, to give you an expected end.

(Jer. 29:11)

Yea, they turned back and tempted God, and limited the Holy One of Israel.

(Psalms 78:41)

Giving Away Spiritual Things

Just as there are "false beliefs" which can hinder an abundant life, there are also principles which can help spawn an abundant life.

Principle One: Give Money Away.

On a spiritual level, you can give away not only money, but also good ideas, spiritual things, witty inventions, wisdom, and spiritual impartations. Remember, first spiritual things, and then natural things–that's the divine order. A healing problem is first a spiritual problem. A health problem, a money problem, a marriage problem, a thought problem, a race problem is a natural problem.

Principle Two: Giving away Spiritual money is giving away your spiritual things. Paul essentially said, "I give you my spirituals and you can return to me your carnals."

If I have not given you any spirituals things you don't need to give me any carnal things.

(I Cor. 9:11)

When a person has a financial problem, they are really having a money problem at the highest spiritual level, which means they lack good ideas, witty inventions, the ability to use the anointing, and a renewed thought life.

Give away that which is spiritual first! There are many Biblical and other examples of this process.

1. God offered His Son first as a spiritual gift and sacrifice. His Son, Jesus, manifested Himself as a natural and physical body in the earth. In return, God received His son back both spiritually and physically.

2. Abraham first offered his son as a spiritual gift or sacrifice back to God. In return, Abraham received back Isaac as a natural inheritance.

3. The Zarepath woman first gave her dead son up to the man of God because she had already been a spiritual blessing to the prophet, Elijah, by sacrificing her last meal for him. In return, the Zarepath woman's son was resurrected and returned to her alive.

4. The Apostle Paul gave his followers spiritual things, and many of the people returned their money, silver, and gold back to him in appreciation for the spiritual things he imparted.

Giving and receiving go hand-in-hand. Give first on a regular basis and then comes the receiving. Apostle Paul, in Philippians 4:19, even prayed a special prayer for those who gave him special money gifts. He prayed over them,

But my God shall supply all your need according to His riches in glory by Christ Jesus.

5. The U.S. Federal Government cannot provide all of its social services to U. S. citizens until the taxpayers first give their taxes. Only then can the Federal Government return money to the various states for social services.

6. When we opened up The Church in College Hill in 1986, on the first day, my wife, Coleen Winburn, and I had to first give $10,000 in the offering before we started a capital campaign for a new building program. We had $500 in the church treasury. At that time, we owned no corporate real

estate. Today, that corporate real estate is worth millions as a result of us giving first our spirituals to the people, and then our carnal money.

7. If one desires a baby in the natural, the man first must release the seed to the egg, and then the return of the baby in the natural will happen.

First give the seed; second, receive the return.

The divine order is giving first, then receiving.

Self-Talk Sabotage

If consciously, or through your self-talk, you mouth some of the statements listed below, it is an indication of why you have no more money, or very little material money, to circulate. The attitudes reflected in these statements will hinder the money-flow process in your life if you are saying things like:

"I don't have any money."
"Money is hard for me to get."
"I have a problem attracting money."
"I've got to hold onto the little money I have."
"That's all the money I've got."
"Don't they know I don't have any money."
"Yes, I am broke, but money isn't everything."
"Money seems to leave me quickly."
"Money is not that important to me."
"I have spent all of my money."
"Money is evil."
"Money just slips through my fingers."
"No matter what I do, I just can't seem to prosper."
"Those rich people are going to hell."
"I can't afford to give the tithe and offerings."
"I am destined to be poor."
"I am jealous of those who prosper and have money."
"You must be doing something wrong to get that kind of money."

"I have a great spirit, but not much money."

"I just want to get to heaven; I don't need money."

"It's a shame that all those pastors, bishops, apostles and television evangelists have all that money."

Do any of those statements sound like you? If so, your words are hindering God's flow of funds into your life! Until you change your thoughts and resistance against money and people, you won't have very much money to help you or others.

Change your thought life and you change your money life.

Finally, at this spiritual dimensional stage, as you change your thought life, it will cause spiritual growth to happen for you through the anointing. Your new thought life will stimulate creative thinking, activate creative faith and imagination, assist with decision making and focus, redirect thought patterns, and move you into breakthrough thinking and focus. Your new thought life will help you chart a vision, and bring you into innovation and new opportunities of the spirit, transforming your soul and body, and stirring up your motivational gifts.

You can stimulate good money ideas through great thoughts.

The Money of the World

Material money is the world's god.

We do not want to obtain money the way the world obtains money. Most of the world's money comes through greed, lust, pride, and ungodly competition. But you and I are going to receive the transfer of our financial wealth through the release of the anointing and character.

Dr. Marcus Hester, in his book *The God Factor*, quotes Rick Joyner's book, *Leadership Management and the Five*

Essentials for Success. Joyner states "Economics is now the most important force dictating <u>political changes</u>. The economic power base is now more powerful than military, religion, or political influences. Economic leadership is what the President must now have." Dr. Marcus Hester then states, "Whoever controls the economic sector will also have power over the religious sector, the political system, and the military."

Releasing the Money Anointing is the apostolic or "sending forth" of God's anointing upon you so you can go forth in the world with your money anointing, being a blessing to others and to the apostolic work in the marketplace.

I strongly recommend that each person who reads *Releasing the Money Anointing* also purchase The Global Inc. book, *An Atlas of the Multinational Corporation* by Medard Gabel and Henry Bruner (2003, Medard Gabel and Toynbee Prize Foundation ISBN1-56584-727-X). Reading their book in its entirety will assist you in using your power of imagination (visualizing) some of the financial wealth in the world. This book will also give you an opportunity to dream. While you read this book, use your creative forces to come up with ideas for business opportunities and entrepreneurship. This is one of the best books I have ever read on understanding the globalization of money, and for charting the financial revenues of multinational corporations.

Gabel and Bruner present a visual representation of multinational corporations and globalization, demonstrating that there is no scarcity of money or wealth in the world. It will expand your thinking and thoughts on money and the Kingdom, helping you see the big picture. They report:

> **The global corporation is an increasingly important economic force in the world.** *With more than 63,000 multinational enterprises and 821,000 foreign subsidiaries, multinational*

corporations directly employ about 90 million people (more than 20 million are in the developing world) and pay more than $1.5 trillion in wages, contribute 25% of the gross world product, and pay more than $1.2 trillion in taxes to the governments of the world—as well as produce much of the goods and services that have raised global standards of living. Out of the 63,000 multinational corporations in the world, the 1,000 largest account for 80% of world industrial output. The Fortune Global 500 alone had more than $45 trillion in assets, $14 trillion in revenues, $667 billion in profits, and about 47 million employees in 2000. Total revenues for the Global 500 increased 10.8 % over the past year while profits climbed 20.4%."

The Force of Change

Moab hath been at ease from his youth, and he hath settled on his lees, and hath not been emptied from vessel to vessel, either hath he gone into captivity: Therefore his taste remained in him, and his scent is not changed.

Therefore, behold, the days come, saith the Lord, that I will send unto him wanderers, that shall cause him to wander, and shall empty his vessels, and break their bottles.

(Jeremiah 48:11-12)

The force of change is here and it is a part of God's New **Transformative Paradigm** for you. This change will help you empty out the old, and move you to another place in the spirit, helping you break out of captivity and tradition. It will change your taste for spiritual things, and change your scent from the old wine to the new wine, moving you from an old vessel to a new vessel, promoting and advancing you into the Kingdom of God.

God is forcing things upon you <u>so you can grow</u>!

God is <u>putting pressure</u> on you so you can come into greater revelation of Him!

It is your decision, your choice, to adapt or adjust to this change or pressure. This is a Godly change to move you out of the state of average, mediocrity, stagnation, and traditional comfort. As a result of this pressure or change, there will come a great <u>spiritual</u>, <u>financial</u> and <u>divine</u> health release in your life!

This change or pressure is going to wean you off of many things, off of many people, and off of all human life support systems. You will stop depending upon certain people for your support. God will give you <u>new friends</u>, <u>new projects</u>, <u>new money</u> , <u>new wealth</u>, <u>new environment</u>, <u>new atmosphere</u> and a <u>new climate</u> for success!

The right response to the force of change is key to your complete thought transformation. You could faint because pressure or change has occurred, you can despise or complain, or you can endure pressure or change.

Your correct response will determine your sonship. Pressure and change is for your edification and growth.

> *And ye have forgotten the exhortation which speaketh unto you as unto children, My son, despise not thou the chastening of the Lord, nor faint when thou are rebuked of him: For whom the Lord loveth he chasteneth, and scourgeth every son whom he receiveth. If ye endure chastening, God dealeth with you as with son; for what son is he whom the father chasteneth not? But if ye be without chastisement, whereof all partakers, then are ye bastards, and not sons.*
>
> (Hebrews 12:5-8)

Things are not going to be the same again because God wants to do a new thing.

Behold, I will do a new thing; now it shall spring

forth; shall ye not know it? I will even make a way in the wilderness, and rivers in the desert.

(Isaiah 43:19)

CHAPTER TWO

The Mystery of the Anointing:

Ask your heavenly Father to reveal the mystery
of the anointing to you right now.

This book will answer the questions, "What is the
Anointing?" and "How can I receive this invisible anointing
so I can become the joint heir that I am to be in the earth?"

A mystery is something that has been hidden from you.
Now it is going to be revealed. Once you have it, you can
walk in the anointings.

In this chapter, we will focus on the mystery of the
anointing.

You were created before the foundation of the world, but
you were not anointed before the foundation of the world.
After you receive Jesus Christ you must press into the
anointing through the baptism of test and a consecrated
life.

The DNA Anointing

"Releasing" means "setting at liberty" or "discharging
that anointing within you" to help you convert the spiritual
into the natural as you walk in heavenly places. All things
are first natural and then spiritual, or in reverse, first
spiritual and then natural. The tabernacle of Moses,
although a natural building, is a type and shadow of that
which is a spiritual pattern of Christ, the Anointed One,
and His anointing.

For example, discharging the anointing within you can
bring forth healing, deliverance, wisdom, money or

materials for you and others through the release of the anointing. However, coupled with your faith, the anointing gives you the ability to convert spiritual things into natural things.

Revelation is spiritual, meaning you first see it spiritually. For example, you first see in the realm of the Holy Spirit your healing or your money.

Transformation is spiritual. You are changed by what you see as you renew your mind in the Word. Because your mind is renewed, you now can handle what you see.

Manifestation is natural, meaning that you can have it now. What has been promised or provided to you by God is first spiritual.

The anointing of God within you is to help you to convert that revelation and transformation into the manifestation of the physical realm.

The Anointing is like a special DNA that smears your life all over. The anointing releases oil upon you for liberty to move you into your greater destiny. This special DNA anointing is passed down from generation to generation from God. This generational linage of the anointing started with God Himself. The DNA anointing is in the seed of God passed down from the Father, the Son and the Holy Spirit.

You are the good seed of God.

He answered and said unto them, He that soweth the good seed is the Son of man; The field is the world; the good seed are the children of the kingdom; but the tares are the children of the wicked one;
                                                    (Matthew 13:37-38)

The seed of God can utilize the anointing of God for the release of divine health, wisdom, money, and prosperity of the soul and body. As the seed of God, you can use the healing anointing, preaching anointing, prophetic anointing, and a money anointing.

According to the Internet encyclopedia *Encarta*,

DNA is better known as deoxyribonucleic acid, and is defined as genetic material of all cellular organisms and most viruses. DNA carries the information needed to direct protein synthesis and replication. Protein synthesis is the production of proteins needed by the cell or virus for its activities and development. Replication is the process by which DNA copies itself for each descendent cell or virus passing on the information needed for protein synthesis. In most cellular organisms, DNA is organized on chromosomes located in the nucleus of the cell.

This Divine Needed Anointing called (DNA) carries information, releases itself, passes on information for revelation, transformation and manifestation. This divine anointing is more powerful than human, animal or plant DNA! Finally, the *Encarta Encyclopedia* discloses the following about DNA:

Studies of human DNA are revealing genes that are associated with specific diseases, such as cystic fibrosis and breast cancer. This information is helping physicians to diagnose various diseases, and it may lead to new treatments. For example, physicians are using a technology called chimeraplasty, which involves a synthetic molecule containing both DNA and RNA strands, in an effort to develop a treatment for a form of hemophilia.

Forensic science uses techniques developed in DNA research to identify individuals who have committed crimes. DNA from semen, skin, or blood taken from the crime scene can be compared with the DNA of a suspect, and the results can be used in court as evidence.

DNA has helped taxonomists determine evolutionary relationships among animals, plants, and other life forms. Closely related species have more similar DNA than do species that are distantly related.

But scientists have not been able to identify or examine this oil called the divine anointing. You must come to know the God of this universe to tap into the four dimensions of the anointing of God. There can be no genetic manipulation of the anointing because you cannot put it under a microscope.

This anointing is similar to human DNA in that it has a unique and specific design for your personality. We can refer to the anointing as a special DNA (Divine Needed Anointing) that gives you an extra boost in life for release of all spiritual things into the physical realm.

This divine, anointed DNA can manifest in your life, giving you your own unique expression, your own set of spiritual fingerprints and distinction, your own signature or seal, your own way of demonstration of the spirit, and your own creative imagination and ways of doing things.

Moses Became a Natural Apothecary of the Anointing

And thou shalt make it an oil of holy ointment, an ointment compound after the art of the apothecary: it shall be an holy anointing oil. And thou shalt anoint the tabernacle of the congregation therewith, and the ark of the testimony, And the table and all his vessels, and the candlestick and his vessels, and the altar of incense, And the altar of burnt offering with all his vessels, and the laver and his foot. And thou shalt sanctify them, that they may be most holy: whatsoever toucheth them shall be holy. And thou shalt anoint Aaron and his sons, and consecrate them, that they may minister unto me in the priest's office. And thou shalt speak unto the children of Israel, saying, This shall be an holy anointing oil unto me throughout your generations. Upon man's flesh shall it not be poured, neither shall ye make any other like it, after the composition of it: it is holy, and it shall be holy unto you. Whosoever compoundeth any like it, or whosoever putteth any of it upon a stranger, shall even be cut off from his people. And the LORD said unto Moses, Take unto thee sweet spices, stacte, and onycha, and galbanum; these sweet spices with pure frankincense: of each shall there be a like weight: And thou shalt make it a perfume, a confection after the art of the apothecary, tempered together, pure and holy:

(Exodus 30:25-35)

And he made the holy anointing oil, and the pure incense of sweet spices, according to the work of the apothecary.

(Exodus 37:29)

Moses learned how to make the Holy Anointing Oil as an offering unto the Lord. Moses used elements to make oils, such as myrrh, sweet cinnamon, calamus, cassia and a portion of olive oil. Moses demonstrated the natural to show us the spiritual in the building of the Tabernacle of God.

The anointing is key to flowing from one point to another. The anointing also brings revelation to help move us from the Outer Court, the First Dimension of grace to the Inner Court, the Holy Place, the Second Dimension of Grace, the Church, and into the Most Holy Place, the Third Dimension of Grace, the Kingdom of God. Mark Hanby refers to the Tabernacle of Moses in three dimensions of grace (I credit him for this teaching, knowledge and understanding of the Tabernacle).

The making of oil by Moses is a type and shadow of how the Shemen of God would work in their lives. Shemen is the Old Testament Hebrew word for anointing. The making of oil in the natural was a similitude of what God was doing through this Shemen anointing upon the people of God. God anointed the children of Israel with Shemen.

And of cassia five hundred shekels, after the shekel of the sanctuary, and a hin of oil olive.

(Exodus 30:24)

The oil here means Shemen. In this passage, the oil (anointing) shows both the spiritual and natural aspects of God and man.

Understand that the Kingdom of God is both spiritual and natural. God demonstrates Himself as both deity and humanity. You have been anointed to help bring about this Godly revolution in the earth. Moses wanted to show God how thankful he was by making oil and incense, pure and holy before the Lord of the tabernacle.

You Can Become a Spiritual Apothecary of the Anointing

The apothecary is a producer of oil. The apothecary knows how to mix the incense of prayer with the four elements of the anointing of God, bringing about a demonstration of God in the earth, blessing others.

You are that spiritual tabernacle of God!
You are that producer of oil in the earth!

Become an apothecary whereby you understand and know how to use and produce the Shemen, Christos, Pneuma and Rhema anointings in your life, and in the lives of others. These four anointings of God are all compounded in one anointing to bring about the explosion and revolution you need to become a transformer of righteousness in the earth.

Releasing the Money Anointing is the result of the anointing, as is healing, wisdom, preaching and teaching.

The cause is the anointing, and the results follow the cause.

All anointing comes from Shemen–the Father–which has its own stamp. Christ–the Christos Anointing–has its own spiritual fingerprint and stamp. The Rhema Anointing–the Word–has its own fingerprint and stamp. The Pneuma

Anointing—the Spirit Anointing—has its own spiritual fingerprint and stamp. These four dimensional anointings each have their own spiritual blueprint, strategy, purpose, maneuvers, and method for making, doing, or accomplishing destiny in your life. The four dimensional anointings are all from the self same God, but operate uniquely and specifically in your life to the degree of your consecrated life of faith.

Every person should desire and experience continually this Divine Needed Anointing (DNA).

The Four Anointings

There are four major types of God-source anointings that manifest in four unique ways. They are as follows:

1. *Shemen* Anointing:
     Shemen is a Hebrew word for anointing.

2. *Christos* Anointing:
     Christos is a Greek Word for "the Messiah, the Anointed One and His Anointing."

3. *Pneuma* Anointing:
     Pneuma is the Greek Word for "Spirit Anointing."

4. *Rhema* Anointing:
     Rhema is the Greek word for "utterance" and "anointing."

God is trying to get money to you. This book will enable you to learn how to receive it.

The Shemen Anointing

And it shall come to pass in that day, that his burden shall be taken away from off thy shoulder, and his yoke from off thy neck, and the yoke shall be destroyed because of the anointing (Shemen).
(Isaiah 10:27)

77

The Shemen anointing is one of those diversities of operations of God, an anointing that operates on several different levels.

And there are diversities of operations, but it is the same God which worketh all in all.

(I Corinthians 12:6)

The Shemen anointing anoints you as prophet, king or priest. It anoints you as a prophet to see, as a king to rule and reign, and as a priest to serve in the sanctuary of the Lord.

The Shemen anointing provided King David with a headship anointing as a captain or priest. David said,

Thou preparest a table before me in the presence of mine enemies: thou anointest my head with oil; my cup runneth over.

(Psalm 23:5)

God has not stopped anointing His people with Shemen. Shemen was good for David, and it should also be good for you today. King David's three natural anointings are a reflection of the Shemen anointing that David received in spirit. First, the natural, then the spiritual.

Shemen also means "to smear and rub on." That is why oil so easily sticks to your skin. David's first natural anointing occurred in the midst of his brethren.

And the LORD said unto Samuel, How long wilt thou mourn for Saul, seeing I have rejected him from reigning over Israel? Fill thine horn with oil, and go, I will send thee to Jesse the Bethlehemite: for I have provided me a king among his sons.

And he sent, and brought him in. now he was ruddy, and withal of a beautiful countenance, and goodly to look to. And the LORD said, Arise, anoint him: for this is he. Then Samuel took the horn of oil, and

anointed him in the midst of his brethren: and the Spirit of the LORD came upon David from that day forward. So Samuel rose up, and went to Ramah.

(I Samuel 16:1,12,13)

David's second natural anointing was when he was placed over the house of Judah.

And the men of Judah came, and there they anointed David king over the house of Judah. And they told David, saying, That the men of Jabeshgilead were they that buries Saul. Therefore now let your hands be strengthened, and be ye valiant: for your master Saul is dead, and also the house of Judah have anointed me king over them. And the time that David was king in Hebron over the house of Judah was seven years and six months.

(2 Samuel 2:4,7,11)

David's third natural anointing occurred as king over all Israel.

Then came all the tribes of Israel to David into Hebron, and spake, saying, Behold, we are thy bone and thy flesh. Also in time past, when Saul was king over us, thou wast he that leddest out and broughtest in Israel: and the Lord said to thee, Thou shalt feed my people Israel, and thou shalt be a captain over Israel. So all the elders of Israel came to the king to Hebron; and king David made a league with them in Hebron before the Lord: and they anointed David king over Israel. David was thirty years old when he began to reign, and he reigned forty years. In Hebron he reigned over Judah seven years and six months: and in Jerusalem he reigned thirty and three years over all Israel and Judah.

(2 Samuel 5:1-5)

A Satanic Anointing?

There is also a satanic anointing which includes

witchcraft, casting spells, magic, corruptions, luck and lying.

> *For many deceivers are entered into the world, who confess not that Jesus Christ is come in the flesh. This is a deceiver and an antichrist.*
>
> (2 John 1:7)

The spirit of the antichrist is an evil spirit. This satanic anointing is a counterfeit, fabricated anointing, an opponent to the Anointed One and His Anointing. The Spirit of the antichrist is an evil spirit that is "anti" the anointing of Christ...it is against Christ.

This evil spirit is a negative anointing.

It is possible to operate in both a godly anointing and a satanic anointing. That is why the Body of Christ is so confused. Many local fellowships operate in a satanic anointing and call it God.

Some of the negative anointings from the spirit of the antichrist include:

The Anointing of Sexual Addiction.
The Anointing of Poverty.
The Anointing of Failure.
The Anointing of Sickness.
The Anointing of Infirmity.

Satan: False Apostle of the Anointing

> *For such are false apostles, deceitful workers, transforming themselves into the apostles of Christ. And no marvel; for Satan himself is transformed into an angel of light.*
>
> (II Corinthians 11:13-14)

Satan is a transformer of a false anointing that looks like and counterfeits the real Christ anointing. The devil can anoint you to do many good things which are not of God. It may be good, but not God. When people embrace the satanic powers, they can do many things that look like God, but are not. It's sad to say that the church has embraced some of the beliefs of this smearing of satanic oil. Some Judeo-Christians practice these things and call it God. They are as follows:

1. Telepathy
   Extrasensory awareness of the thoughts or actions of others.

2. Telekinesis
   Movement of objects without material cause.

3. Tantra
   Discovering one's Buddha nature.

4. Astral Projection
   Leaving the physical body and traveling to another location or reality.

5. Divination
   a. The art or practice that seeks to foresee or foretell future events or discover hidden knowledge usually by the interpretation of omens or by the aid of supernatural powers.

   b. Unusual insight: intuitive perception.

Who has Anointed You?

I often hear people in the Body of Christ say, "He is an anointed preacher." "She is an anointed singer." The real question should be, "Who has anointed them, Satan or God?"

For example, a preacher or singer can work in and out of these opposing anointings. The anointing of Satan one day, and the anointing of God another day. It depends on what cup they are drinking from that particular day...the cup of the Lord or the cup of the devil.

Ye cannot drink the cup of the Lord, and the cup of devils: ye cannot be partakers of the Lord's table, and of the table of devils.

(1 Corinthians 10:21)

You must work hard not to be smeared or rubbed with a negative, satanic anointing by submitting yourself to the Word of God. Renew your thoughts and you won't have a satanic anointing.

Wherefore by their fruits ye shall know them.

(Matthew 7:20)

Dr. D. K. Olukoya, in his book, *Criminals in the House of God,* states:

One of the most horrible things that can happen to a person is for two opposite spirits to be operating in the person's life. It is a fearful thing. (There is a positive anointing and a negative anointing.) Nevertheless, it is true. This is what we call negative anointing. When it falls upon a person, the person gets under evil influences.

Why is it that an addicted person does not get better?

Perhaps they are operating with an evil anointing, trying to live a double life. One day they are in God, the next day they are working for the devil. This is called a satanic anointing.

Wherefore by their fruits ye shall know them. Not every one that saith unto the me, Lord, Lord, shall enter in the kingdom of heaven; but he that doeth the will of my Father, which is in heaven. Many will say to me in that day, Lord, Lord, have we not prophesied in thy name? And in thy name have cast out devils? And in thy name done many wonderful works? And then will I profess unto them, I never knew you: depart from me, ye that work iniquity.

(Matthew 7:20-23)

Satan was anointed from the beginning.

Thou art the anointed cherub that covereth and I have see thee so thou wast upon the holy Mountain of God; Thou hast walked up and down in the midst of the stones of fire.

(Ezekiel 28:14)

Satan has corrupted the anointing of God and created his own fabricated anointing, which is negative thoughts. Satan is still anointed. He can make you financially rich and wealthy through this false or fabricated anointing. But his ultimate goal is to destroy you.

God, through His Shemen and Christos anointings, can help you to create wealth and abundance, building you up for the Kingdom of God so you can be a blessing to others and the apostolic work of God in the earth.

God or Satan as Source?

There are three major sources of anointings. There is only one power and that is the power of God. Satan has no power unless you give him power, or activate his power.

God as a source of anointing is called Shemen.

Satan as a source of anointing is called the negative thought anointing, a fabricated anointing, a counterfeit anointing given by the anointed cherub (the devil).

Either God is your source, Satan is your source or there is a worldly anointing. It is possible for Satan to assist someone in becoming financially wealthy. Not all financial wealth or money is obtained by God as the source. If you cut a deal with Satan, you can become financially wealthy and have temporary health, but Satan will ultimately destroy you, using you up and burning you out. You can cut a deal with the devil, the "queen of heaven," but you will pay with your spirit, soul, and body.

Therefore pray not thou for this people, neither lift up cry nor prayer for them, neither make intercession to me: for I will not hear thee. Seest thou not what they do in the cities of Judah and in the streets of Jerusalem? The children gather wood, and the fathers kindle the fire, and the woman knead their dough, to make cakes to the queen of heaven, and pour out drink offerings unto their gods, that they may provoke me to anger.

(Jeremiah 7:16-18)

But we will certainly do whatsoever thing goeth forth out of our own mouth, to burn incense unto the queen of heaven, and to pour out drink offerings unto her, as we have done, we, and our fathers, our kings, and our princes, in the cities of Judah, and in the streets of Jerusalem: for then had we plenty of victuals, and were well, saw no evil. But since we left off to burn incense to the queen of heaven, and to pour out drink offerings unto her, we have wanted all things, and have been consumed by the sword and by the famine.

(Jeremiah 44:17-22)

And there came one of the seven angels vials, and talked with me, saying unto me, Come hither; I will shew unto thee the judgment of the great whore that sitteth upon many waters: With whom the kings of the earth have committed fornication, and the inhabitants of the earth have been drunk with wine of her fornication. So he carried me away in the spirit into the wilderness: and I saw a woman sit upon a scarlet coloured beast, full of names of blasphemy, having seven heads and ten horns. And the woman was arrayed in purple and scarlet colour, and decked with gold and precious stones and pearls, having a golden cup in her hand full of abominations and filthiness of her fornication: And upon her forehead was a name written, MYSTERY, BABYLON THE GREAT, THE MOTHER OF HARLOTS AND

*ABOMINATIONS OF THE EARTH. And I saw the
woman drunken with the blood of the saints, and
with the blood of the martyrs of Jesus: and when I
saw her, I wondered with great admiration.*

(Revelation 17:1-6)

The Mind of the Anointing

The Christos Anointing is the anointed mind of Christ
mingled with your mind, with your unseen healing,
deliverance and money.

Let this mind be in you, which was also Christ (the
Anointed One and His Anointing) *Jesus. Let this
mind of the anointing be also in you.*

(Philippians 2:5)

Ask Christ to smear, rub and oil your mind with His Mind!

Dr. O. K. Olukoya, in his book, *Slaves Who Love Their
Chains Shall Remain in Their Bondage*, states,

*The anointing is the supernatural equipment that
enables an ordinary human being to achieve
supernatural results. The anointing is a divine
electric force. Once that divine electric force comes
upon you it shocks your entire system.*

Your entire spirit and entire mind is flooded with
newness.

Once you become anointed, it also provides a special
protection upon your life. Touch not my anointed, and do my
prophets no harm. This anointing is not automatic...you
must press into it with a life of character, consecration, and
a holy lifestyle.

This anointing comes from God, Christ, the Spirit, and
the Word.

Dr. Olukoya further states that the power of the anointing is the demonstration of the raw power of God.

The anointing makes you to do what flesh and blood cannot do. The anointing is the demonstration and expression of God that brings about results without sweat.

The anointing is the demonstration and expression of God Himself, Christ Himself, the Holy Ghost Himself, and the Word Himself.

A Worldly Anointing

God can anoint you, Satan can anoint you or the world can anoint you for abundance, wealth, and money. A worldly anointing comes from having a love for the world system. You believe that your money, wealth and abundance will come from the world system as your primary source. There are millions of people who depend on the world as their source. They can use the following worldly philosophy and doctrines to become quite wealthy with money and materials without belief in the God of Abraham. Millions of people are wealthy because they have learned how to work the world system. In some cases they have sold themselves to the world. They are owned by the world system. The world system has become their god. Money is their god.

Listed below are philosophies that the world embraces:

1. Humanism

A philosophy that usually rejects supernaturalism and stresses an individual's dignity, worth, and capacity for self-realization through reason.

2. Materialism

A preoccupation with, or stress upon, material rather than intellectual or spiritual things.

3. Consumerism

    a. The promotion of the consumer's interests.

    b. The theory that an increasing consumption of goods is economically desirable; also, a preoccupation with an inclination toward buying consumer goods.

How Do You Receive this Anointing?

How do you possess the anointing for everything that God has promised you in the Word?

This anointing comes through:

1. Character Development.
2. Consecration.
3. Sanctification and Holy Lifestyle.
4. Prayer.
5. Obedience.
6. Discipleship training.
7. Moving from just a believer to a disciple and from a disciple to a Son of God.
8. Being fathered by a spiritual father.
9. The Baptism of temptations, trials and test.

Wherefore holy brethren, partakers of the heavenly calling consider the Apostle and High Priest of our profession, the Anointing (Christ-Jesus).

(Hebrews 3:1)

Seeing then that we have a great high priest, that is passed into the heavens, Jesus the Son of God, let us hold fast our profession. For we have not an high priest which cannot be touched with the feeling of our infirmities; but was in all points tempted like as we are, yet without sin. Let us therefore come boldly unto the throne of grace that we may obtain mercy, and find grace to help in time of need.

(Hebrews 4:14-16)

But the natural man receiveth not the things of the Spirit of God: for they are foolishness unto him: neither can he know them, because they are spiritually discerned.

(1 Corinthians 2:14)

The natural man is "governed" only by his environment and situation, and by his natural instincts. He sees things after the first Adam, and operates in the fallen Adamic nature. We originally came from God because we were made after the image and likeness of God. The second Adam redeemed us back to this image and likeness of God.

Being saved does not guarantee you the anointing automatically. Being baptized in the Holy Ghost does not guarantee the anointing. The special anointing is reserved for the sons of God and the children of promise (the seed of promise).

The anointing of God is in the unseen realm.

For our light affliction, which is but for a moment, worketh for us a far more exceeding and eternal weight of glory; while we look not at the things which are seen, but at the things which are not seen: for the things which are seen are temporary; but the things which are not seen are eternal.

(2 Corinthians 4:17-18)

The anointing is the eternal stuff of God; you cannot see it with your natural eyes (that's the mystery of it).

But we speak wisdom of God in a mystery, even the hidden wisdom, which God ordained before the world unto our glory: which none of the princes of this world knew: for had they known it, they would not have crucified the Lord of glory. But as it is written, Eye hath not seen, nor ear heard, neither have entered into the heart of man, the things which God hath prepared for them that love him. But God hath revealed them unto us by his Spirit: for the

Spirit searcheth all things, yea, the deep things of God.

(1 Corinthians 2:7-10)

The anointing brings you into the deep things of God, revealing to you the hidden wisdom of God in a mystery. The anointing of God searches all things and brings you into the deep things of God. Because of the anointing, you will begin to experience:

A.   Deep revelation and mysteries.
B.   Deep transformations of God to change situations and circumstances.
C.   Deep manifestations of God.
D.   Deep demonstrations of God in the Earth.

You will do things others will not be able to do. When others get tired, you will have the strength to go on and move ahead with dynamite and regeneration. You will be able to accomplish much more than others who have burned out. Others will be baffled by your strength and energy because you know how to use the four major anointings of God: Shemen, Christos, Pneuma and Rhema.

The Deep Things of God

But God hath revealed them unto us by his Spirit: for the Spirit searcheth all things, yea, the deep things of God.

(1 Corinthians 2:10)

The Spirit of God within you brings together both Shemen and Christos anointings, so you can receive greater messages, greater revelations through your recreated human spirit. Your mind is not capable of receiving these depths of the anointing...they are given by His Spirit to your recreated human spirit.

You may ask, "What does all this 'deep calleth into deep' mean?"

It means that as you consecrate your life, the anointing will be communicated to you in dimensions and depths that only He will do for the sons and daughters of God. The depth of the anointings will help you stay updated and current with the things of God in both heaven and earth.

You will constantly receive a fresh word on the Church, the Kingdom of God, the nation, the economy, when no one else has a word. But you will know the orchestrations of God in part in both heaven and earth because you are connected and linked to the deep things of God.

Stewards of the Mysteries of the Anointing

Let a man so account of us, as of the ministers of Christ, and stewards of the mysteries of God.
(1 Corinthians 4:1)

We are stewards of the mysteries of these four anointings. The majority of the Body of Christ does not understand this because they are not flowing in the anointing. Most of the Body of Christ is going through the motions.

You and I are appointed to be ministers of the anointing!

Holding the mystery of the faith in a pure conscience.
(1 Timothy 3:9)

You and I hold the mystery of the faith in pure conscience.

The Indwelling Anointing

The anointing now rests upon you because you have learned how to tap into the dimensions of Christ, the Anointed One and His Anointing.

The indwelling anointing brings you into the freedom in the Spirit.

Once-and-for-all you have no more hang-ups about anything. You have no more idiosyncrasies about money, wealth, obedience, riches, abundance, or prosperity. You are now free in spirit, soul and body!

What shall we then say to these things? If God be for us, who can be against us?

(Romans 8:31)

There is now therefore no condemnation to those who are in the anointing (Christ the Anointed One and His anointing). The anointing freed us from the law of sin and the second death, bringing you into the things of the Spirit. The anointing gives you life and peace.

The spirit of the anointing dwells in you to activate your recreated human spirit, bringing life and righteousness. The anointing brings about resurrection and takes you out of corruption, making you a joint heir with Christ the Anointed one and His anointing.

The anointing helps the development of your sonship and the ultimate redemption of your body, both in heaven and earth. It activates Christ's intercession for you before God, helping you to achieve your calling and destiny.

The Anointing Will Teach You

You must receive unction from the Holy One and you will know all things. You need to know about money, healing, and glory. This unction is the anointing from the Holy One.

They went out from us, but they were not of us; for if they had been of us, they would no doubt have continued with us: but they went out, that they might be made manifest that they were not all of us. But ye have an unction from the Holy One, and ye know all things.

(1 John 2:19-20)

Once you receive the anointing and the anointing dwells in you, you will not need man to teach you as much about Releasing the Money Anointing. **This book will hopefully anoint your spiritual eyes with salve so you can see in the realm of the spirit.**

I counsel thee to buy of me gold tried in the fire, that thou mayest be rich; and white raiment, that thou mayest be clothed, and that the shame of thy nakedness do not appear; and anoint thine eyes with eye slave, that thou mayest see.

(Revelation 3:18)

Once you grasp this teaching, and your spiritual eyes are open, the Holy Spirit will continue to show you how to grow in obtaining money to bless others.

Two Glories

The anointing will bring you into two types of glory:

1. The glory as to come into the presence of God.

For I reckon that the sufferings of this present time are not worthy to be compared with the glory which shall be revealed in us.

(Romans 8:18)

For it became him, for whom are all things, and by whom are all things, in bringing many sons unto glory, to make the captain of their salvation perfect through sufferings.

(Hebrews 2:10)

2. The glory as to experience the prosperity that will be placed upon your life.

Arise, shine; for the light is come, and the glory of the LORD is risen upon thee.

(Isaiah 60:1)

For the LORD God is a sun and shield: the LORD will give grace and glory: no good thing will he withhold from them that walk uprightly.

(Psalm 84:11)

The anointing will teach you all the things you need to know about money, wealth, abundance, and faith.

Your problem is not money.
Your problem is not divine health.
Your problem is not divine healing.
Your problem is not wealth or abundance.
Your problem is a lack of, or no anointing of God.

You need the character of the anointing of God to release all the money and materials coming to you.

The anointing has been set aside for the sons and daughters of God; for those who seek the face of God. When you seek His face, you create a wealthy place of His presence-the place of His glory, or the third dimension of grace. Everything you need such as money, wealth, abundance...will come from the source of this anointing: the Father Himself, the God of Shemen.

When you release your anointing, you will receive money, favor, material goods, good relationships, customers, and healing.

The anointing will allow you to enter your rest, your joy, righteousness, and peace in the Holy Ghost. You will receive the God-kind of happiness. The more you submit to the authority of the Lord God, the greater the release of the anointing in your life.

CHAPTER THREE

Administration and Operation of the Anointing

The mystery of the anointing includes one source, but different administrations and operations for Shemen, Christos, Pneuma and Rhema. Each anointing has its own distinct personality, diversity and administration, but all flow from the self-same Spirit or source...the God-kind of source.

From a natural perspective, I am one person or one source. For example, I am a husband, and I have an anointing for my wife. I am a father, and I have an anointing for my children. I am an Elder/Bishop, and I have an anointing for the local corporate church through shepherd rule and bishop rule. I am a son of God, and I have an anointing for my brothers and sisters.

My personal administration and operation for each anointing has its own personality, distinction and differences. For example:

1. With my wife I do not operate like a father.
2. With my two daughters I do not operate as their husband.
3. With the local apostolic fellowship where I am a set man, I do not operate as a husband over the fellowship. Instead, I operate as an elder or bishop in the fellowship.

To understand administrations and operations, you must realize that God anoints in four different ways, but all flow from the same self-source.

Anointing One
The *Shemen* Anointing:

Administration and Operation

The *Shemen* anointing of God is one type of anointing. This is the Father's anointing. All Old Testament anointing was *Shemen* anointing. As a New Testament people, we are entitled to all four levels of anointings in our life. The deeper we go into our life with God, the deeper the level of anointings.

> *And it shall come to pass in that day, that his burden shall be taken away from thy shoulder, and his yoke from thy neck, and the yoke shall be destroyed because of the anointing (Shemen).*
> (Isaiah 10:27)

> *Then Samuel took a vial of oil, and poured it upon his head, and kissed him, and said, Is it not because the LORD hath anointed thee to be captain over his inheritance?*
> (I Samuel 10:1)

> *Then Samuel took the horn of oil, and anointed him in the midst of his brethren: and the Spirit of the LORD came upon David from that day forward. So Samuel rose up, and went to Ramah.*
> (I Samuel 16:13)

> *Thou preparest a table before me in the presence of mine enemies: thou anointest my head with oil; my cup runneth over (Anointest my head with Shemen).*
> (Psalm 23:5)

> *But my horn shalt thou exalt like the horn of an unicorn: I shall be anointed with fresh oil (Oil is Shemen here).*
> (Psalm 92:20)

> *To appoint unto them that mourn in Zion, to give unto them beauty for ashes, the oil of joy for*

mourning, the garment of praise for the spirit of heaviness; that they might be called trees of righteousness, the planting of the LORD, that he might be glorified (Oil is Shemen here).

(Isaiah 61:3)

Anointing Two
The Christos Anointing:

Administration and Operation

The *Christos* anointing of Christ is a second type of anointing. This is the Son's anointing.

Therefore leaving the principles of the doctrine of Christ, let us go on unto perfection; not laying again the foundation of repentance from dead works, and of faith toward God.

(Hebrews 6:1)

There is therefore now no condemnation to them which are in Christ Jesus, who walk not after the flesh, but after the Spirit.

(Romans 8:1)

Anointing Three
The Pneuma Anointing:

Administration and Operation

The Pneuma anointing of the Spirit is a third type of anointing. This is the Holy Spirit's anointing.

For I know that this shall turn to my salvation through your prayer, and the supply of the Spirit of Jesus Christ.

(Philippians 1:19)

And my speech and my preaching was not with enticing words of man's wisdom, but in demonstration of the Spirit and of power.

(1 Corinthians 2:4)

He therefore that ministereth to you the Spirit, and worketh miracles among you, doeth he it by the works of the law, or by the hearing of faith?

(Galatians 3:5)

The Lord Jesus Christ be with thy spirit. Grace be with you. Amen.

(2 Timothy 4:22)

Anointing Four
The Rhema Anointing:

Administration and Operation

The *Rhema* anointing of the Word is the fourth type of anointing. This is the anointing that comes from the Word, and every word that proceeds out of the mouth of God.

But what saith it? The word is nigh thee, even in thy mouth, and in thy heart: that is, the word of faith, which we preach.

(Romans 10:8)

So then faith cometh by hearing, and hearing by the Word of God.

(Romans 10:17)

That he might sanctify and cleanse it with the washing of water by the word.

(Ephesians 5:26)

In the beginning was the Word, and the Word was with God, and the Word was God.

(John 1:1)

Each anointing of God takes you into deeper levels and dimensions with God, Christ, the Spirit, and the Word.

The Christos anointing took the Apostle Paul into the third heaven. When Apostle Paul was caught away to the third heaven, he received special visions and revelations of

God.

The anointing of Christ will permit you to see special visions of God.

> *How that he was caught up into paradise, and heard unspeakable words, which it is not lawful for a man to utter.*
>
> (2 Corinthians 12:4)

Domestic Transference of the Anointing

1 Corinthians 11:13 states:

> *But I would have you know that the head of every man is Christ, and the head of the woman is the man, and the head of Christ is God.*

As a husband I have a transference anointing to my wife and family.

Men, we must stop trying to get our wives to submit to our personalities. The wife should only submit to the anointing. If a husband does not possess any Christos anointing, it is going to be hard for his wife to submit or to subject themselves to his authority.

In the domestic realm, Christ is my head, meaning He is the authority over me. His anointing is given to me to the degree that I am in submission to my head (Christ). As I submit to Christ, my head in the marriage, this anointing is released upon me to be distributed to my wife and children.

Wives, read this next part very carefully!

From a spiritual perspective, my wife is not submitting to me or my personality, she is really submitting to the anointing of Christ that has been distributed to me as a husband as I submit to my head, Christ, in the domestic order.

In other words, I can anoint my wife and children with this Christos anointing to the degree that they are willing to obey and submit to my anointing which has been given to me by my husband or head, Christ. The problem with ninety percent of Christian marriages is that the husband is not submitted to Christ, and therefore, Christ cannot anoint that marriage.

When the wife will not submit to her husband's anointing, there is no oil flowing in her life for the marriage to survive the attacks of others and the devil. That marriage is not covered and has no protection. Therefore the wife and the children have no oil for their lamps. There is no anointing flowing in that marriage, so the marriage dies. We must work hard to keep oil in our marriage.

I know this teaching on releasing the money anointing is a strange teaching to those who do not spend time living in the realm of the spirit (the unseen realm). If you spend most of your time living in the realm of the earth you will be earthly, but not spiritual.

Witness Nee, in the *New Testament Recovery Version Bible*, states the following about the Apostle Paul:

Revelation is the putting aside of the veil, the unveiling of hidden things: vision is the scene, the view, seen at the unveiling. Many things concerning God's economy and administration in the universe were hidden. The Lord revealed, unveiled these to the Apostle, and he received visions of these hidden things.

So when you get anointed with Shemen, you are a candidate for Christos anointing, then you can be anointed with the Pneuma anointing which takes you right into the Rhema anointing of the Word.

God has much to say about His heavenly economy that He is revealing to His apostles through the anointing.

Once you learn the depth of each one of these anointings, you will be able to discern when someone is ministering under the Father's anointing, the Son's anointing, the Holy Spirit's anointing or the Word's anointing.

A person may be a gifted, talented preacher or singer, but not an anointed preacher or singer. There is a huge difference!

The Anointing of Spirit Beings

The entire Kingdom of God is based on the release of the anointing of God upon the spirit beings below.

1. God anointed Lucifer (an outlawed angel) who ultimately corrupted his anointing by getting out of order or out of place.

2. God anointed the two major angels who, to this day, obey Him. God also has special angels who carry healings in their wings. These angels carry an anointing for healings. These angels have oil in their wings.

3. God anoints mankind that seeks Him.

The anointings are reserved for those who seek a deeper relationship with Him.

The Two Anointed Ones
(The Angelic Anointing)

Then answered I, and said unto him, What are these two olive trees upon the right side of the candlestick and upon the left side thereof? And I answered again, and said unto him, What be these two olive branches which through the two golden pipes empty the golden oil out of themselves? And he answered me and said, Knowest thou not what these be? And I said, No, my lord. Then said he, These are the two anointed ones,

that stand by the LORD of the whole earth.
                                    (Zechariah 4:11-14)

The two angels in Zechariah 4:11-14 possessed the anointings of God. These angels are prophetic seers and watchers. They are the two sons of oil.

These are the two olive trees, and the two candlesticks standing before the God of the earth.
                                    (Revelation 11:4)

There are two olive trees, two sons of the anointing, which are called angels. These angels are involved with the process of oil and the circulation of oil as demonstrated in their emptying of oil.

They report back to our heavenly Father what is going on in the earth. These anointed angels are also linked to other angels who watch and monitor what is going on in each local fellowship or church throughout the world.

No one is getting away with anything!

Pastors and bishops who have failed to obey God are not getting away with anything. The watchers have reported it.

That is why they are called "watchers" in the earth. These watchers take note and document everything that is going on in life of the House of God by reporting back to heaven about the status of the House of God.

And he dreamed, and behold a ladder set up on the earth, and the top of it reached to heaven: and behold the angels of God ascending and descending on it. And, behold, the LORD stood above it, and said, I am the LORD God of Abraham thy father, and the God of Isaac: the land whereon thou liest, to thee will I give it, and to thy seed; And thy seed shall be as the dust of the earth, and thou shalt spread abroad to the west, and to the east, and to the north, and to the south: and in thee and in thy seed shall all the families of the earth be blessed. And, behold, I am with thee, and will keep thee in all places whither thou goest, and will bring thee again into this land; for I will not leave thee, until I have done that which I have spoken to thee of. And Jacob awaked out of his sleep, and he said, Surely the LORD is in this place; and I knew it not. And he was afraid, and said, How dreadful is this place! This is none other but the house of God, and this is the gate of heaven.

(Genesis 28:12-17)

The anointing is also going to be released by the Spirit of God (the Pneuma of God). Zerubbabel made it clear how our lives should be led. The Spirit of God will take us into the anointing of God.

Then he answered and spake unto me, saying, This is the word of the LORD unto Zerubbabel, saying, Not by might, nor by power, but by my spirit, saith the LORD of hosts.

(Zechariah 4:6)

And the angel that talked with me came again, and waked me, as a man that is wakened out of his sleep. And said unto me, What seest thou? And I said, I have looked, and behold a candlestick all of gold, with a bowl upon the top of it, and his seven lamps thereon, and seven pipes to the seven lamps, which are upon the top thereof: And two olive trees by it, one upon the right side of the bowl, and the other upon the left side thereof. So I answered and spake to the angel that talked with me, saying, What are these, my lord? Then the angel that talked with me answered and said unto me, Knowest thou not what these be? And I said, No, my lord. Then he answered and spake unto me, saying, This is the word of the LORD unto Zerubbabel, saying, Not by might, nor by power, but by my spirit, saith the LORD of hosts. Who art thou, O great mountain? before Zerubbabel thou shalt become a plain: and he shall bring forth the headstone thereof with shoutings, crying, Grace, grace unto it. Moreover the word of the LORD came unto me, saying, The hands of Zerubbabel have laid the foundation of this house; his hands shall also finish it; and thou shalt know that the LORD of hosts hath sent me unto you. For who hath despised the day of small things? for they shall rejoice, and shall see the plummet in the hand of Zerubbabel with those seven; they are the eyes of the LORD, which run to and fro through the whole earth. Then answered I, and said unto him, What are these two olive trees upon the right side of the candlestick and upon the left side thereof? And I answered again, and said unto him, What be these two olive branches which through the two golden pipes empty the golden oil out of themselves? And he answered me and said, Knowest thou not what these be? And I said, No, my lord. Then said he, These are the two anointed ones, that stand by the LORD of the whole earth.

(Zechariah 4:1-14)

The Role of the Anointed Angels

Bless the LORD, ye his angels, that excel in strength, that do his commandments, hearkening unto the voice of his word. Bless ye the LORD, all ye his hosts; ye ministers of his, that do his pleasure. Bless the LORD, all his works in all places of his dominion: bless the LORD, O my soul.

(Psalm 103:20-22)

Who maketh his angels spirits; his ministers a flaming fire:

(Psalm 104:4)

And he saith unto him, Verily, verily, I say unto you, Hereafter ye shall see heaven open, and the angels of God ascending and descending upon the Son of man.

(John 1:51)

The angel of the LORD encampeth round about them that fear him, and delivereth them.

(Psalm 34:7)

Know ye not that we shall judge angels? how much more things that pertain to this life?

(1 Corinthians 6:3)

Christ's anointing is greater than the angels:

Being made so much better than the angels, as he hath by inheritance obtained a more excellent name than they.

(Hebrews 1:4)

Hebrews 1:7-9 speaks of angelic spirits:

And of the angels he saith, Who maketh his angels spirits, and his ministers a flame of fire. But unto the Son he saith, Thy throne, O God, is forever and ever: a sceptre of righteousness is the sceptre of thy kingdom. Thou hast loved righteousness, and hated iniquity; therefore God, even thy God, hath anointed thee with the oil of gladness above thy fellows.

(Hebrews 1:7-9)

Angels move around us most of the time. Some are as strangers.

Be not forgetful to entertain strangers: for thereby some have entertained angels unawares.

(Hebrews 13:2)

The decree of the watchers (angels):

This matter is by the decree of the watchers, and the demand by the word of the holy ones: to the intent that the living may know that the most High ruleth in the kingdom of men, and giveth it to whomsoever he will, and setteth up over it the basest of men.

(Daniel 4:17)

Angels are ministering spirits.

Are they not all ministering spirits, sent forth to

minister for them who shall be heirs of salvation?
                                                    (Hebrews 1:14)

Angels can stand at the gates of a city.

And had a wall great and high, and had twelve gates, and at the gates twelve angels, and names written thereon, which are the names of the twelve tribes of the children of Israel:
                                                    (Revelation 21:12)

Questions You May Have on How to Release the Anointing

1. Would you like to be so anointed that others would be able to touch you in a godly way and be healed and delivered?

2. Would you like to be so anointed that you can change the atmosphere and environment everywhere you go?

3. Would you like to be so anointed that your presence could bring about a godly conviction in those around you?

4. Would you like to be so anointed that you are able to raise the dead?

Well it is possible for you!

The release of these special anointings is demonstrated in the lives of many men and women of God throughout the Bible:

1. The Release of the Anointing through His Shadow.

The Apostle Peter had so much anointing that people who fell out and under his shadow were healed.

Insomuch that they brought forth the sick into the streets, and laid them on beds and couches, that at the least the shadow of Peter passing by might overshadow some of them. There came also a multitude out of the cities round about unto

Jerusalem, bringing sick folks, and them which were vexed with unclean spirits: and they were healed every one.

(Acts 5:15-16)

2. The Release of a Protective Anointing.

King David revealed that it is dangerous to wrongly handle those who are anointed.

Saying, Touch not mine anointed, and do my prophets no harm.

(Psalm 105:15)

3. The Release of the Anointing is Not For Sale.

There are some people who are willing to pay for the anointing of the Holy Spirit. Neither the anointing nor the Holy Spirit are for sale. You must come through Christ as a first step to receive the anointings.

And when Simon saw that through laying on of the apostles' hands the Holy Ghost was given, he offered them money, Saying, Give me also this power, that on whomsoever I lay hands, he may receive the Holy Ghost.

(Acts 8:18-19)

4. The Release of the Anointing to Open Spiritual Eyes.

Elisha was so anointed that he prayed immediately that his servant's eyes would open in the realm of the spirit, and his servant was able to see the reinforcements of God to win the battle.

And he answered, Fear not: for they that be with us are more than they that be with them. And Elisha prayed, and said, LORD, I pray thee, open his eyes, that he may see. And the LORD opened the eyes of the young man; and he saw: and, behold, the mountain was full of horses and chariots of fire round about Elisha. And when they came down to him, Elisha

*prayed unto the LORD, and said, Smite this people,
I pray thee, with blindness. And he smote them with
blindness according to the word of Elisha. And
Elisha said unto them, This is not the way, neither is
this the city: follow me, and I will bring you to the
man whom ye seek. But he led them to Samaria.*

(2 Kings 6:16-19)

5. The Release of the Anointing to Shake a Building.

Apostle Peter and Apostle John were so anointed that
the place was shaken where they were assembled.

*And when they had prayed, the place was shaken
where they were assembled together; and they were
all filled with the Holy Ghost, and they spake the
Word of God with boldness.*

(Acts 4:31)

6. The Release of a Singing Anointing.

The singing from the Apostle Paul and Silas had so much
of an anointing that while they were singing the following
happened:

*   Suddenly there was a great earthquake.

*   Chains broke off the prisoners because of this
    anointed singing (without musical instruments).

*   The jail door opened automatically.

*   The jailer met Christ, the Anointed One and His
    anointing at midnight and got saved.

*And at midnight Paul and Silas prayed, and sang
praises unto God: and the prisoners heard them. And
suddenly there was a great earthquake, so that the
foundations of the prison were shaken: and
immediately all the doors were opened, and every
one's bands were loosed. And the keeper of the prison
awaking out of his sleep, and seeing the prison doors*

open, he drew out his sword, and would have killed himself, supposing that the prisoners had been fled. But Paul cried with a loud voice, saying, Do thyself no harm: for we are all here. Then he called for a light, and sprang in, and came trembling, and fell down before Paul and Silas, And brought them out, and said, Sirs, what must I do to be saved? And they said, Believe on the Lord Jesus Christ, and thou shalt be saved, and thy house.

(Acts 16:25-31)

7. The Release of the Anointing for Healing.

Jesus released an anointing that healed them all.

And the whole multitude sought to touch him: for there went virtue out of him, and healed them all.

(Luke 6:19)

8. The Release of a Money Anointing.

Christ the anointed One and His anointing used His anointing to locate money in the mouth of a fish. Christ and the apostles did not have money in their possession at the time to pay taxes. However, Jesus used His anointing to find a piece of money.

And when they were come to Capernaum, they that received tribute money came to Peter, and said, Doth not your master pay tribute? He saith, Yes. And when he was come into the house, Jesus prevented him, saying, What thinkest thou, Simon? of whom do the kings of the earth take custom or tribute? of their own children, or of strangers? Peter saith unto him, Of strangers. Jesus saith unto him, Then are the children free. Notwithstanding, lest we should offend them, go thou to the sea, and cast an hook, and take up the fish that first cometh up; and when thou hast opened his mouth, thou shalt find a piece of money: that take, and give unto them for me and thee.

(Matthew 17:24-27)

109

You should have the anointing to do what you have to do when you need to do it. Although Christ did not have money with Him, He did have the anointing of Shemen (God with Him) to call forth money. The anointing of God is not just for those who possess it. The anointing of God is to be a blessing to others. Always keep this in mind: we are anointed to bless others.

9. The Release of an Activation Anointing of a Dead Body.

The part that is anointed first is your re-created human spirit. Your soul and your body can directly benefit from this anointing. The Prophet Elisha had so much anointing residing on his body that when they took him out to the cemetery to bury him, that anointing residing on his body rubbed up against another dead body and the dead body stood up.

And it came to pass, as they were burying a man, that, behold, they spied a band of men; and they cast the man into the sepulchre of Elisha: and when the man was let down, and touched the bones of Elisha, he revived, and stood up on his feet.

(2 Kings 13:21)

The anointing can be released in every area of your life. There are many areas of your life where the anointing can affect you, such as:

a. The release of the divine healing anointing.
b. The release of the prophetic anointing.
c. The release of the spiritual warfare anointing.
d. The release of the prayer anointing.
e. The release of the faith anointing.
f. The release of the psalmist anointing.

g. The release of entrepreneurship anointing.
h. The release of the money anointing.

You may also be used as a vessel for the Manifestation of the Spirit to operate. When the four anointings of God is activated in your life, the following may result:

a.   The word of wisdom.
b.   The word of knowledge.
c.   Faith.
d.   Gifts of healing.
e.   Working of miracles.
f.   Prophecy.
g.   Discerning of spirits.
h.   Divers kinds of tongues.
i.   Interpretation of tongues.

Now there are diversities of gifts, but the same Spirit. And there are differences of administrations, but the same Lord. And there are diversities of operations, but it is the same God which worketh all in all. But the manifestation of the Spirit is given to every man to profit withal. For to one is given by the Spirit the word of wisdom; to another the word of knowledge by the same Spirit; To another faith by the same Spirit; to another the gifts of healing by the same Spirit; To another the working of miracles; to another prophecy; to another discerning of spirits; to another divers kinds of tongues; to another the interpretation of tongues: But all these worketh that one and the selfsame Spirit, dividing to every man severally as he will.

(1 Corinthians 12:4-11)

Repeat after me the following confession:

I am so thankful for the anointed God who commingles my recreated human sprit with His anointing, the anointed Christ who commingles my recreated human spirit with His anointing, the anointed Spirit who commingles my recreated human spirit with His anointing, and the anointed Word which commingles my recreated human spirit with His anointing.

CHAPTER FOUR

One-Thousand Fold Anointing!

The LORD God of your fathers make you a thousand times so many more as ye are, and bless you, as he hath promised you!

(Deuteronomy 1:11)

Poverty is of the devil, from the very pit of hell and from bad thoughts.

Poverty loves company. Poor people hang together. Poverty is not just the reverse of wealth. In the book, Poverty Must Die, published by Battle Cry Christian Ministries, the point is made that poverty can include:

1. Poverty of the Spirit.
2. Poverty of achievement.
3. Poverty of good health.
4. Poverty of good ideas.
5. Poverty of money.
6. Poverty of lack of influence.
7. Poverty of godly relationships.

Poverty can make criminals. Some rich people steal too! There are also rich criminals. People steal thinking that they are going to get something they need; instead, they get a jail cell.

Poverty is a spirit and poverty is a thought. However, we should not put people down by mocking them. Proverbs 17:5 says we should help poor people to understand that they can be anointed to come out of poverty. We should do all we can to help the poor according to Proverbs 28:27.

Satan has blinded the minds of believers to think that

there is something holy about being poor. The spirit of poverty makes you afraid to give to the Kingdom of God.

He therefore that ministereth to you the Spirit, and worketh miracles among you, doeth he it by the works of the law, or by the hearing of faith?
(Galatians 3:5)

We all have the ability to actually minister the spirit of the Lord to each other! Christ—the anointed One—is on the inside of us, so we have His anointing abiding in us so we can minister to people the spirit of the Lord.

He is in me and He is in you.

When I write about the release of money through your life, there is an anointing. In fact, there is a spiritual anointing for everything you need—for deliverance, for prophecy, for your money—from the realm of the spirit, the unseen realm of the Spirit of God. **God is using me through this book to minister His financial anointing to you by the Spirit, and to break the spirit of poverty** and bad thoughts.

Beloved, I wish above all things that thou mayest prosper and be in health, even as thy soul prospereth.
(3 John 2)

John is writing about prospering in spirit, soul and body. God wants you to walk this earth without depression, oppression, or repression. He wants you to walk with your head up, never melancholy, because the greater One is inside of you! Make a choice to walk in joy, righteousness, and peace in the Holy Ghost.

It is God's will for your mind and emotions to prosper, to rise above nervous conditions and mental problems.

You'd Better Like Silver and Gold!

Revelation 21 (the entire chapter) speaks about silver, gold and pearls in heaven. Friend, if you do not like money, stay away from heaven!

And the building of the wall of it was of jasper: and the city was pure gold, like unto clear glass.

(Revelation 21:18)

Also see Proverbs 8:18, Psalms 105:36 and Isaiah 45:3.

Get your spirit ready to experience the one-thousand fold anointing!

No more settling for the thirty, sixty, one hundred fold...God wants you to experience the thousand-fold anointing. Your money is being released to you right now in the spirit just by the reading of this book. **God is using this book to cause a corporate anointing to move upon His Church.** In the Spirit, start receiving your prosperity and wealth. God wants to make you a spiritual money magnet where money follows you. Once you absorb this teaching, you are going to find yourself having more wisdom, more skill, more knowledge, more money, more riches and abundance than you have ever had before.

But my God shall supply all your need according to his riches in glory by Christ Jesus.

(Philippians 4:19)

The Greek word for supply here is *pleroo* which means "to make full, to fill up," like filling a prescription. God, through Christ, is filling a prescription to meet your financial needs. The Holy Spirit is going to bring about a release of the anointing through you to have money, riches, and prosperity. Through His anointing, it is almost impossible for you not to experience healing, deliverance and material abundance. You won't be able to help yourself.

The sick, the poor, the depressed need the anointing to ask for breakthrough.

For verily I say unto you, That whosoever shall say unto this mountain, Be thou removed, and be thou cast into the sea; and shall not doubt in his heart, but shall believe that those things which he saith shall come to pass; he shall have whatsoever he saith.

(Mark 11:23)

115

The flow of health and riches will come because the anointing of the Holy Spirit saturates every aspect of your life. Your money, your healing, is going to come by the Spirit. Your healing comes by the spirit of faith. Your deliverance comes by the spirit of faith. Your answered prayers come by the spirit of faith.

Why are you afraid to release your money through the unseen spirit-realm of faith?

"Money Isn't Important To Me"

Do not go to work tomorrow and see what happens. Load up a basket of groceries at the store and fail to pay for it and see what happens.

Money matters.

You need money to buy clothes, groceries, transportation, lodging...to further the Kingdom.

There is a spiritual supply for every need. The work of the Holy Spirit is going to activate your money. How can this happen?

Trust in the LORD with all thine heart; and lean not unto thine own understanding.

(Proverbs 3:5)

It is not your job to tell the Holy Ghost how to do it. Just trust God. Acknowledge Him in all your ways. The anointing carries a special money supply for every need.

But thou shalt remember the LORD thy God: for it is he that giveth thee power to get wealth, that he may establish his covenant which he sware unto thy fathers, as it is this day.

(Deuteronomy 8:18)

Let this Scripture do more than inform you, let it transform you. God gives you the power to get wealth because He knows you function better with money than you do when you are broke, busted, and disgusted. The power to live a healthy life, the power to love, the power to have money, is important to us all.

Money is important.

I am not writing on materialism. You can be a materialist and be without God. And, you can be a Christian and be involved in materialism, and not be involved with the anointing that produces what you need in the earthly realm.

The God of Abraham, Isaac and Jacob, and the God of Charlie Winburn wants to give you the power to flow wealth into your life. He gives you the anointing to destroy every financial yoke.

And it shall come to pass in that day, that his burden shall be taken away from off thy shoulder, and his yoke from off thy neck, and the yoke shall be destroyed because of the anointing.

(Isaiah 10:27)

You are of Abraham's covenant and entitled to receive the fruitful riches of the promises God made to Abraham.

The Purpose of Wealth?

God wants to establish His Kingdom covenant in the earth through you. His only eyes are your eyes. His only legs are yours. If God is going to accomplish His purpose in the earth, it will be done through your life.

The purpose of wealth and riches is so you can help establish the covenant of God in the earth.

...that he may establish his covenant which he sware unto thy fathers, as it is this day.

(Deuteronomy 8:18)

Now, look at the preceding verse:

117

*And thou say in thine heart, My power and the might
of mine hand hath gotten me this wealth.*

(Deuteronomy 8:17)

The power, the release, and anointing is in your anointed hands!

The God of Abraham has given your hands the power and anointing to get wealth whether you are educated, skilled, or a professional.

How to Handle the Anointing

The Body of Christ is very unskillful in handling their anointing. They do not know what to do when the anointing comes. You must be open to the Spirit, so God can give you wisdom on how to sit down and count the costs of what you are doing. God will give you wisdom on how to invest and how to sow.

It is your heritage to be wealthy, to enjoy abundance, to experience more than enough. God wants you the head and not the tail. You are Abraham's seed, heir according to the promise.

*And if ye be Christ's, then are ye Abraham's seed, and
heirs according to the promise.*

(Galatians 3:29)

What promise?

The promise He made to Abraham that he should have wealth, finances, abundance, divine health, and healing. All that was promised to Abraham, Isaac and Jacob is yours! Here are just a few of those glorious promises in Deuteronomy 28:

*The LORD thy God will set thee on high above all
nations of the earth...* (verse 1)

*All these blessings shall come on thee, and overtake
thee.* (verse 2)

Blessed shalt thou be in the city, and blessed shalt thou be in the field. Blessed shall be the fruit of thy body, and the fruit of thy ground, and the fruit of thy cattle, the increase of thy kine, and the flocks of thy sheep. (verses 3-4)

Blessed shalt thou be when thou comest in, and blessed shalt thou be when thou goest out. (verse 6)

The LORD shall cause thine enemies that rise up against thee to be smitten before thy face... (verse 7)

The LORD shall command the blessing upon thee in thy storehouses, and in all that thou settest thine hand unto... (verse 8)

The LORD shall establish thee an holy people unto himself. (verse 9)

All people of the earth shall see that thou art called by the name of the LORD; and they shall be afraid of thee. (verse 10)

Thou shalt lend unto many nations, and thou shalt not borrow. (verse 12)

The LORD shall make thee the head, and not the tail... (verse 13)

Isn't that what you want for your life and family? It is yours as you obey God. (I suggest you read verses 15-68 to discover the consequences of not making the choice to obey God's Word and change your thoughts).

You choose life or death, blessing or curse, by your obedience or rebellion.

There is a principle called "the law of its own kind," or "the law of draw." Simply stated, rich people hang together. Anointed folk hang together. You never see poor people running with the rich. Everything gravitates toward its own kind. Those who would attempt to undermine the Gospel hang together. I choose to hang with the Abrahamic covenant out of Abraham. We are the generational wealth of God so we obtain riches like silver, gold, or money.

God wants you to turn from opposing yourself.

And it shall come to pass in that day, that his burden shall be taken away from off thy shoulder, and his yoke from off thy neck, and the yoke shall be destroyed because of the anointing.

(Isaiah 10:27)

The yoke shall be destroyed because of the Shemen. This is the Hebrew word for "anointing." It's the Shemen that destroys the yoke. David said he anoints my head with Shemen (Old Testament). The Shemen is the anointing that makes you wealthy in every aspect of your life.

Prophetically speaking, we are in "that day" when burdens will be taken from our shoulders! God wants us to walk in divine health, to walk in His money anointing, so you can release your money anointing through the Kingdom of God.

God wants to remove the burdens of sicknesses such as heart attacks, massive strokes, and cancer.

He wants to remove financial burdens.

God is not the author of poverty, sickness, and spiritual death.

Yokes are bondages holding you down. Many of you have yokes of financial debt, yokes of house problems, transportation problems. But the Bible says these yokes shall be destroyed because of the anointing (shemen).

Do not Eat the Seed

If you want to experience God's harvest, do not eat the seed. When you get fifty, one hundred, or one thousand dollars in your hand, that could be **the initial seed for you to sow a portion of that money back.** If you have been believing God for two thousand dollars, then return your tithe, give the offering, and then sow a seed. Give three hundred or four hundred dollars as your special seed so that you will be able to sow an "uncommon" seed of $1,000, $5,000, $10,000 or even $100,000.00!

I just recently gave a $1,000 seed to Mike Murdock Ministries. That seed unlocked a $103,000 uncommon seed for me and my family to return to the Apostolic ministry in Cincinnati. That $103,000 unlocked millions to help construct our new Prayer Center, Training Auditorium and state-of-the-art Child Care Center.

Do not eat the seed.

The seed you receive is going to bring the harvest of bigger money.

Seed comes in all kinds of ways. And when the seed comes, never turn it down.

We have a sister in our fellowship who runs a daycare. Her rates for this service are extremely reasonable because she wants to be a blessing to people. But I feel guilty just giving her what she charges. One time she kept our children for two days, six hours each day. I thought to myself, "I am going to have to fuss and fight with her to pay her what she should charge." I knew in advance she would not receive the money I wanted to pay her.

When I gave her a huge financial seed, she said, "I just can't receive that."

I reminded her of Luke 6:38. "God is going to get money to you through other people."

The anointing will attract the right people to give financially to you. Even those who do not like you will give when the anointing is released on you and

through you.

She ultimately accepted the money because she had been praying, asking God for extra money. In essence, she had placed a demand on the anointing that was her heritage. In the spirit, she had been believing God for His promise.

That unexpected money became a seed she could sow, reinvesting it into the Kingdom of God and supporting the work of the Apostles.

The money I gave to my children's caretaker came to me from a brother in our fellowship who gave me an envelope for my birthday. I had prayed, "Lord, I put a demand on some money to bless this sister." Jesus put a demand on His anointing to find the money in the fishes' mouth to pay His taxes. Right then and there the money appeared. When I opened that envelope, I had the seed money to plant into her life.

I put a demand on my anointing, and God touched this man's heart to release the anointing in him to give to me so I would have money to bless the sister right then and there!

You need to give.

Sow a seed into a television, radio or other Apostolic outreach ministry to help expand their sphere of influence. Your seed will release the greater anointing for the greater overflow for the greater abundance.

BIG financial wealth is coming through you.
BIG financial abundance is coming.
BIG financial favor is coming.

The anointing is coming to unclog your financial veins so your money can constantly flow all the time.

Part of your plan to learn to flow in His anointing is to locate and read all the Scriptures on the anointing. Let these Scriptures sink into your spirit until they no longer are information, but become spiritual seed for transformation and manifestation.

Our Practical Plan
to Release the Anointing

Our fellowship is developing a one-stop shop business resource center to train our people how to walk in wealth and release God's anointing in their lives.

There will be an investment division to help people invest in stocks, bonds and CDs, and a real estate division teaching our people how to find and purchase real estate. There will also be a division to help our people obtain their real estate licenses.

We plan to have a division that helps people market their products and services through award-winning business plans. We will also help people learn how to create money in interstate and networking commerce.

We selected these areas because every millionaire I know derived their wealth from these five major areas: investment, real estate, developing a small business, and the Internet or networking and financial seed sowing.

Another division will train and develop entrepreneurs in leadership and business management, teaching them the tools for success. Still another division will deal with capital fund raising—how to expand business through venture capital, public offerings, loans, credits and Internet finances. And, how to manage your cash flow.

One special initiative division will open up our own cosmetology school, with a beauty salon right next to it; then we will establish a barber school. We also plan to open up a daycare business—as well as a state-of-the-art health club.

We plan to establish a credit management center, and help people establish home-based businesses. There will also be an estate planning division. Our people will be creating so much money they will need someone to help them prepare their taxes and plan their estates.

Our fellowship is collectively growing in the understanding that God will flow His financial anointing through our lives when we decide to seek it, obey His laws, and create the realization that, as the seed of Abraham, it is our heritage and blessing.

CHAPTER FIVE

"Increase On God's Mind"

So then faith cometh by hearing, and hearing by the Word of God.

(Romans 10:17)

Because you have heard does not mean you have received. The just shall live by faith.

Now faith is the substance of things hoped for, the evidence of things not seen.

(Hebrews 11:1)

Hearing it once does not mean you own it. "I heard that" does not mean you possess it. Are you tired of just believing and never receiving what you believe?

That's why, at the end of the last chapter, I encouraged you to look up all the references in Scripture concerning the anointing, then read them over and over until His Word becomes part of your spirit so your inner self is strengthened and supercharged.

You may not have much now, but if you walk in these principles, it is coming to you and through you!

Though thy beginning was small, yet thy latter end should greatly increase.

(Job 8:7)

Although you have started out small, and it may have taken you years to get what little you have, God can turn that situation around overnight, in the twinkling of an eye. Dr. Creflo Dollar states, "God has increase on His mind," and since we are His children, increase should be on our minds.

Let me clarify that. John says,

He must increase, but I must decrease.

(John 3:30)

That Scripture refers to serving each other, but does not refer to finances. In the context of money and finances, God has increase on His mind for you!

God wants you to increase in the spirit, increase in your mind, increase in your body, increase in your finances, increase in wisdom, increase in wealth, and increase in abundance!

To reach God's desire, we must renew our minds. Create new thoughts.

There are three foundational truths to receive the power to get wealth.

Truth One:

The releasing of the money anointing is based on one major premise: <u>God is your source</u>.

You do not need any of the world's instruments for power and wealth when you have the anointing. The anointing extracts your money from the world. God can create wealth, even touching other peoples' hearts to bless you. In fact, if God is not the source of your riches and wealth, you will be miserable!

Truth Two:

<u>It is your choice to be wealthy or poor</u>.

Please note that when we talk about wealth, we are not just talking about money. You can have wealth without having much money. However, sooner or later, as you walk in abundant thinking, you will experience God's promises for your life.

You can decide not to be wealthy, not to be prosperous,

126

not to experience abundance or surplus. But, God gives everyone the same opportunity to receive these things. You will find out later you are the wealth of God.

God has already given these things through you. Now it is up to you to choose life or death, poverty, or wealth. God will never force His wealth on you.

I have heard Christians say, "Well, I do not need to have wealth or much money."

That's their choice. However, the Bible says that the wealth of the wicked is laid up for the righteous! This means...

...the wealth of the sinner [finds its way eventually] into the hands of the righteous, for whom it was laid up.

(Proverb 13:22, Amplified)

If that money is designated by God for the righteous, but the righteous do not want it, then the unrighteous will continue to rule by using the money that divinely belongs to us.

Whatever state you are in financially, materially, or physically, you created it yourself. You may not like that, but it is true. If you are poor and broke, you are responsible unless you are in an oppressive country that controls the poor through evil, or territorial oppression. America is a great and prosperous country, I am glad I live in America.

Truth Three:

If you choose poverty or wealth, <u>you cannot blame others for the results</u>.

If you possess wealth, it did not come just through other people. You received your wealth through God's anointing. If you are poor, stop blaming the devil or God. You are poor because you believe you are destined to be poor. Your thoughts got you your poverty.

There are countries oppressed by ungodly governments that stifle prosperity, but you do not live there, you live in America! Pray for the oppressed, bless the poor, send money to missions.

And, better yet, you have the Holy Spirit to lead and guide you in all truth, even into wealth, prosperity, and abundance.

You are poor because you are blaming somebody else. Welfare? The governor? The President?

Instead, blame yourself or your very bad thoughts.

This is the word of the LORD unto Zerubbabel, saying, Not by might, nor by power, but by my spirit, saith the LORD of hosts.

(Zechariah 4:6)

Do You Have the Spirit of Poverty?

They were first taught by Dr. Creflo Dollar, so I am quoting, paraphrasing and crediting him. There are several tests to determine if you have the spirit of poverty. I have great confidence in Creflo Dollar's anointing as God has released it in this man's life. Although I've never met him personally, I do subscribe to many of his teachings, including his ways to know if you have the spirit of poverty. Although you may have the anointing of God in your life, for some reason your money will not flow. Something is holding it up. I'm convinced it is due to thinking or thoughts.

For as he thinketh in his heart, so is he:.

(Proverbs 23:7)

You are who you think you are.

We know who God is, but many do not accept who God

says we are. If you are thinking anything other than what God has said about you, your thinking is going to be faulty.

Look at these tests to examine your thinking to discover if you are creating a spirit of poverty in your life through your thoughts.

Test one:

Do you try and justify where you are, and justify why you cannot give?

Well, I've always been like this. I'll never change. I'll always be poor.

Poverty is a curse. Frankly, I pray and act better when all my needs are met and I can bless somebody else. My spirit is lifted when I have more than enough to be a blessing to others.

Poverty is from your thoughts and your bad thoughts will never prompt you to give money into the Kingdom of God.

If the spirit of the Lord comes upon you to give, do it. Do not question, "Was that God, the devil, or me?" You know it can't be the devil, and if it is you, so what? You have a desire in your heart to plant a seed because you have the inner voice of your recreated human spirit.

Do not wait to "hear God." God is a giver, and as a pattern son, you need to give. Give because He first loved you by giving His only begotten Son, the dearest, most precious thing to Him...so that you might have life more abundantly.

Test Two:

Are you afraid to give under the direction of the Holy Spirit?

Do you govern your finances with a lack of trust about God as your source for the anointing?

You cannot pick and choose when you want Him to be your source of anointing. You cannot play the lottery or gamble at the race track and say, "God is my source."

Do you govern your finances through a lack of trust about God? Settle it in your heart that God is your source.

Test Three:

Are you suspicious, governed by the fear of others taking your money?

You need to give, you need to give to unlock God's process to flow money into your life! And do not be afraid that preachers will try to take your money. They do not need your money. You are the one that needs to give so God and others can get money, materials, and favor back to you.

Give, and it shall be given unto you; good measure, pressed down, and shaken together, and running over, shall men give into your bosom. For with the same measure that ye mete withal it shall be measured to you again.

(Luke 6:38)

God uses other people to bless you financially, favoring you with contracts, favoring you with promotions, favoring you with business opportunities.

I beseech you therefore, brethren, by the mercies of God, that ye present your bodies a living sacrifice, holy, acceptable unto God, which is your reasonable service. And be not conformed to this world: but be ye transformed by the renewing of your mind, that ye may prove what is that good, and acceptable, and perfect, will of God.

(Romans 12:1-2)

To release this money anointing, you must constantly renew your mind or your thought life. One week in the fellowship I gave out rubber bands and asked the people to put them on their wrists, snapping them with each negative thought (I got this idea from a book I read, but I do not remember the author who first made this suggestion). This is a simple way to experience that your mind needs to be transformed. Snap the rubber band every time you think a negative thought.

Get your mind right and the truth shall set you free.

Transformation and Manifestation

Present yourself "holy" and God can transform you.

Do not "conform" your thinking on how to get wealth to the world's way, but look to God who has a better way. **His way may be slower, but it is built on a rock that will last.**

Let your mind be transformed every day through God's Word and continuous worship. God is a spirit and they that worship Him must worship Him in spirit and in truth (His Word).

Seek the perfect will of God (either you are in it or you are not). If you are not loving your wife, you are out of God's will. If you are not taking care of your children, and doing what the Bible says as a man of God, you are out of the will of God.

Renew your mind through the washing of the water of the Word each day. Just as you wash your body each day, you need to wash out your mind. You need a clear mind when you get up in the morning because the enemy is going to come in and try to attack your mind. Use the rubber band each day to help you get rid of these negative, crazy thoughts.

Cast not away therefore your confidence, which hath great recompense of reward.

(Hebrews 10:35)

Do not allow the devil to cast away the confidence you have in God because maintaining confidence in Him will produce great rewards after you have done the will of the Father. Ask anything according to His will and He hears! "I do not care what the doctors' say, my confidence is in God." Thank God for the doctors, but they do not have the final word about your life.

Transformation comes through the mind, and manifestation comes in the physical realm.

By staying in the Word, you keep yourself perfect in spirit. Your money is coming by the spirit, and your spirit is 100 percent perfect. God has given your spirit control over your soul and body. You can tell your body to obey in the name of Jesus: "I am not going to eat all of this sugar and carbohydrates."

If you constantly renew your mind, your money anointing will start flowing.

You must understand that money is not anointed. However, one can be anointed to get money to be a blessing to others. Releasing the money anointing is releasing the anointing within you to create the power to get wealth and money.

Wealth and power start in the spirit, in your ability to hear the inner witness of the Holy Spirit.

God is a God of increase and He wants you to be profitable in the earth!

The LORD shall increase you more and more, you and your children.

(Psalm 115:14)

Many Christians still believe the lie that money is evil. Money is not evil! God's Word says the love of money is the root of evil.

For the love of money is the root of all evil:
(I Timothy 6:10)

Someone said, "The real truth is that the lack of money is the root of all evil!" Without money, people steal, sell their bodies, and any other act it takes to obtain money.

Jesus was not poor. He became poor to take on your little poverty. Let me ask you, "What does a poor man need with a treasury?" Jesus had a treasury!

Wealth is more than money.

Wealth also involves a healthy emotional life and good physical health. When your thoughts are right and pure, when you are not thinking evil thoughts about others, then you are wealthy.

God wants you prepared for the wealth transfer that has taken place. Your hands have been anointed for wealth (Deuteronomy 8:17) because God has no problem with silver or gold.

Though your beginning journey to wealth may be small, the Lord will increase you greatly in your latter days. Begin to transform your mind by saying to yourself many times each day, "This is my year to bring in God's abundance."

For 42 days, I want you to faithfully repeat these powerful 42 words the Lord gave me in prophecy a year ago.

I have the blessing.
I have the favor of God.
I have a river of increase.
God is the source of my increase because He dwelleth in me, and He doeth the works
I believe on Jesus and I do greater works

(John 14)

CHAPTER SIX

The Set Time is Now!

Two things will hinder you in walking in the millionaire anointing and attitude:

1. The fear of failure, and...
2. The fear of success.

Some people do not believe they are righteous enough to receive what God has for them. They are afraid of the exposure that prosperity brings.

Friend, you are the righteousness of God! It is your heritage, your divine right to receive His blessings! Because you have right-standing in Him, you can begin to experience "millionaire thinking" and start to express yourself through the anointing.

The spirit of failure is HUGE! It comes upon you and says, "You haven't had much all of your life. All you've had is a job. So what makes you think it will be any different now?"

It will be different because that is God's plan. He is going to release money from the heavenlies through His anointing for you, and that anointing is literally going to be more than you could ever ask or think, more than your expected income, influence, and favor.

To walk in all God has for your life, to walk in a millionaire anointing, you must rebuke that spirit of failure that comes upon you.

Why do you need the money? So that you can be a blessing to the Apostolic work of God in the Earth by bringing many sons of God into glory. Don't be afraid in giving away

135

all of your millions because you can always start over and over again, because of the anointings available to reproduce in your life again.

The Bible says,

> *For as he thinketh in his heart, so is he.*
> (Proverbs 23:7)

Your ungodly thoughts (thoughts that do not line up with God's Word) have hindered you from coming into your abundance and your wealth. It is your "stinkin thinkin" that causes you to be sick, broke, and poor all the time.

> *Beloved, I pray that you may prosper in every way and*
> *[that your body] may keep well, even as [I know] your*
> *soul [emotions] keeps well and prospers.*
> (3 John 2, Amplified)

So, God's desire is for you to abundantly prosper in two major areas: your health and your finances.

God is not blessing His people with sickness. Christ has redeemed us from the curse of the law, and sickness is a curse.

You need to constantly renew your mind in His Word. If you fail to do so, you will be sick, broke, poor, bellyaching, and complaining about your current pathetic condition.

If you are sick for a long period of time, it is a curse. When you get sick, stand on God's Word and get healed!

The reality of life is simply this: there is a spirit of failure and a spirit of success. Decide to walk in the spirit of success. If you do not feel worthy of success, remind yourself that you are one of God's sons, one of the righteousness of God, and God commands men to give to you!

> *Give, and it shall be given unto you; good measure,*
> *pressed down, and shaken together, and running over,*
> *shall men give into your bosom. For with the same*

136

measure that ye mete withal it shall be measured to you again.

(Luke 6:38)

God will send men and women into your life to help you possess new technology in your hands, to help you prosper through the Internet, to train you in the latest technology, to leverage the latest scientific breakthroughs, to profit from biological discoveries, or flourish in foreign affairs.

The moment you decide to accept your heritage of success, heaven opens up and sends somebody to help you!

This is Insanity!

I once heard insanity defined in the following manner: "Insanity is when you keep doing the same things you have always done, yet expect a different result."

Let me rephrase that, Charlie Winburn style:

"If you want to keep getting what you've always got, then keep doing what you've always done!"

No matter how you say it, it is insanity to expect different results from the same old non-productive behavior!

If you keep on doing what you have always done, you will keep on getting what you have always got, and that's nothing. Why do you keep attracting the same old man? Because you keep doing what you have always done, manifesting the same behavior to lure that same old crackpot you have always attracted through your unrenewed mind.

If you want to walk in the spirit of success, then you must abandon what you've always done and said. Forever ban condemning statements from your thinking and your mouth! Stop saying stupid things such as:

"I'm not worthy of success."

"I'll always be sick."

"There's never been any money in my family. My mamma was poor, and now I'm poor. That's the way it will always be."

"Welfare is the only system I've ever known."

"I'm a single mother, so I'll never get ahead."

How can you walk in III John 2 when your "stinkin' thinkin'" stops you, oppresses, and regresses you? God wants your mind, your emotions and your finances to prosper. Let me repeat it again!

> *Beloved, I pray that you may prosper in every way and [that your body] may keep well, even as [I know] your soul [emotions] keeps well and prospers.*
> (III John 2, Amplified)

Do you see it? God wants your emotions to prosper. He wants you to feel good. He wants you to be healthy in your mind, healthy in your emotions, healthy in your intellect, healthy in your body.

I have a monitor on my phone because I cannot allow myself to be bombarded by ungodly thinking. There are certain people who call only when they need to moan and groan about another mess in their lives. The Bible admonishes us to "take heed of what you hear," so I've learned to monitor to whom I talk. In fact, some people wallow in self-pity so deeply that if you entertain their conversations, they can bring you down with them.

Revelations of God from Ephesians 3

> *For this cause I bow my knees unto the Father of our Lord Jesus Christ, Of whom the whole family in heaven and earth is named. That he would grant you, according to the riches of his glory, to be strengthened with might by his Spirit in the inner man; That Christ may dwell in your hearts by faith;*

that ye, being rooted and grounded in love, May be able to comprehend with all saints what is the breadth, and length, and depth, and height;

(Ephesians 3:14-18)

In verse 14, underline the word "Christ," which means "the Anointed One" and His anointing. It is vital that we constantly renew our minds, constantly think the things of God, constantly think on those things which are holy, so we can receive the heritage of "the Anointed One."

Finally, brethren, whatsoever things are true, whatsoever things are honest, whatsoever things are just, whatsoever things are pure, whatsoever things are lovely, whatsoever things are of good report; if there be any virtue, and if there be any praise, think on these things.

(Philippians 4:8)

If you are living in sin, do not be so foolish as to believe that God is going to bring you into an abundance of wealth. It is not going to happen! You need to live a holy, sanctified life, obeying His Word, meditating on the good (God) things, to receive His anointing. You can get wealth through a satanic anointing or worldly anointing. It is your choice!

Ephesians 3:15 explains that you are part of "the whole family in heaven and earth." You are part of your spiritual family in heaven, through eternity, and part of the Body of Christ on earth, united under His Name.

Ephesians 3:16 guarantees that you will be strengthened according to His riches! I pray this book will be used by God to strengthen you up so you can explode in the riches of God.

You do not need to walk in oppression any more. You can cancel that next counseling appointment when you are full of God's glory and put your confidence in God, standing up and trusting Him with all your heart, all your strength, all your soul.

It is time for many reading this book to abandon the welfare mentality that constantly cries "Help me, help me," and instead start to declare... "Through Christ I can do all things."

Ephesians 3:17 tell us that Christ, the Anointed One, releases His anointing to dwell in your heart by faith, "that ye being rooted and grounded in love" may understand. Now go back and re-read verse 14. When you are anointed, you are going to have favor with God and man.

And, in God's anointing, you will be able to comprehend with all the saints (verse 18).

Any time you hear the word "Christ" you need to think about the Anointed One and His anointing. In verse 18, the Apostle Paul is talking about the breath of the anointing for the largeness of your wealth, favor, and money. Largeness will bring about vastness, greatness, extensiveness, and magnitude in your life. Your wealth, abundance, favor, and money are being positioned for you because you are the righteousness of God.

You can get healed with this revelation!

You can become wealthy from this revelation!

There is life in the anointing, and God is going to give you a measure of His anointing for wealth. **God wants to give you a wide span, a huge reach, a large dimension in the anointing.** Start declaring out loud, "I'm going deeper into His anointing, deeper in His glory, deeper in His presence."

If you are overweight, start thinking about a change through His anointing. Your surplus weight will slow you down and hinder what God wants to do through your life. It will rob you of the energy you need in your service to God. Obesity can trigger other health problems, such as diabetes and heart issues. Certainly Jesus never walked the earth with a fat belly, and He even condemned the gluttons. If you are heavy, determine now to get rid of that overweight mentality and start asking God to release His anointing for your total health!

Are you starting to feel this revelation in your spirit? There's a depth to the anointing. God, through Jesus the Anointed One, wants to take you deeper in the things of His Kingdom.

He wants you to increase! Now is your time to rise up and be planted by the rivers of water, to flourish in the courts of our God.

Small Stuff Produces Big Stuff

Though thy beginning was small, yet thy latter end should greatly increase.

(Job 8:7)

Although your beginning may be small, do not despise small beginnings! You are not going to stay small. In the smallness God is testing you because God cannot trust you with the big stuff until you have learned how to handle the small stuff. If God can't trust you to return your tithes and offerings on $3.50, He cannot give you $350,000. But, when He can trust you with the $3.50, then the progression starts. Next He will give you $35.00, then $350.00, then $3,500, then $35,000, then $350,000, and so on. And, if He can trust you with $350,000, He knows He can trust you with $3,500,000.

Our local fellowship was spiritually small in thinking for several years, but now God is making us better because He knows He can trust us. We have proved faithful in our making and molding. He sent us down to the Potter's House where we were circumcised. He cut away our flesh so we could see the Spirit of the Lord revealed.

Your beginning may have been small, but your latter end shall be great!

Your hour has come. You have been tested. Now is your time to come into the hundred-fold, even the thousand-fold blessing.

You may start out in the mail room, then move up to the computer room. As they trust you, you become a manager, and then the treasurer of the corporation. In time, you find yourself a board member, then a vice president with big stock options. After a long time of being faithful, the Board of Directors declare, "We are turning over our $100 million corporation to you because you did not despise small beginnings and have been faithful in all we have given to you."

If we are to take this world for Christ, we need more than enough money, more than enough teaching materials, more than enough favor, more than enough wisdom, more than enough abundant attitude.

We need to be abundant in every way of life: in spirit, soul, and body.

Four Actions for Activating the Anointing

You need to do four things to activate the money anointing:

Action One:

You must <u>believe</u> in the money anointing. The money is not anointed. You are anointed. Keep that in mind.

The Bible, in Deuteronomy 8:18, declares that God gives you a money anointing to get wealth. The word "wealth" means "abundance and prosperity." There are over 463 Scriptures in the Bible that discuss prosperity, abundance, wealth, and money.

Believe that God is the source of your money anointing.

Action Two:

You must <u>believe</u> the money anointing is for you.

It is one thing to believe in the money anointing, and yet another to believe it is for you! Recognize that you are a son of God, and as such, you are an heir to the heritage of Abraham! God's abundant promises are for You!

Action Three:

You must <u>desire</u> the money anointing for your life.

You cannot be afraid of money. You cannot be afraid to be exposed to large amounts of money. It is not evil. Only the "love of money" is wrong. Money takes on the personality of its owner. If you are a good person, your money will be used for good things, including helping further the Kingdom of God. If you are a thief or a crook, you are a thief or crook with money. Money takes on the personality of the owner. Develop a desire for money to meet the needs of your family, and help establish God and His Kingdom on earth.

Action Four:

You must be <u>willing to walk</u> in the money anointing.

After you believe in the anointing, believe it is for you, and desire it, you must be willing to take the steps to walk in it! "Walk in it" means that you are willing to support the Kingdom of God with your finances, and are willing to use your finances to help other people establish God's covenant.

Of the approximately 463 Scriptures dealing with prosperity, 114 are on abundance, 120 are on wealth, and 30 are on money. Do not tell me that your money is not important to God! God declared that He gives you the power to get wealth...abundance, money, favor, healing, deliverance. Do you know anywhere in Scripture where God ever took back what He promised?

> *And if ye be Christ's, then are ye Abraham's seed, and heirs according to the promise.*
>
> (Galatians 3:29)

You are in Christ, so you are Abraham's seed, and therefore are heir to all of His precious promises. Now, get ready for the wealth transfer that is already on the earth (Proverb 13:22). It is not "laid up" anymore. We have it!

But, you must declare it to have it. Just knowing that the wealth is yours is not enough. You must go further. The wealth transfer took place when Jesus came down as a rich man and took on poverty as a poor man so that we can become rich. This is the wealth transfer, the ability to have a full supply of anything in Him!

> *For we know the grace of our Lord Jesus Christ, that, though he was rich, yet for your sakes he became poor, that ye through his poverty, might be rich.*
>
> (II Corinthians 8:9)

The Anointing Attracts Wealth

> *A good man leaves an inheritance of moral stability and goodness to his children's children and the wealth of the sinner finds its way eventually in the hands of the righteous for whom it is lain up.*
>
> (Proverb 13:22, Amplified)

Wealth will eventually find its way into your hands. Your anointing attracts money, healing, deliverance, joy, righteousness, and peace to you.

Money somewhere in the universe is looking for you right now. Money is going to find its way into the hands of the righteous. The sinner is gathering up your money, but you will enjoy it.

He that by usury and unjust gain increaseth his substance, he shall gather it for him that will pity the poor.

(Proverbs 28:8)

Do you see it? The sinner is gathering up your money and your materials for you as a son of God. The poor no longer need to be poor when they come to understand and seek the money anointing.

Make no mistake about this...God will not put His wealth into the hands of a crazy fool involved in sin, lust, greed and stinginess. However, you can get wealth through a satanic anointing or worldly anointing...it is your choice.

For God giveth to a man that is good in his sight wisdom and knowledge and joy but to the sinner He giveth weeping and travail together and to heap up that He may give it to him that is good before God.

(Ecclesiastes 2:26)

If you are good before God, then you stand to inherit the promises of Isaiah 45:3:

I will give thee the treasures of darkness hidden riches of secret places that thou mayeth know that I am the Lord which called thee by thy name.

What are these treasures of darkness?

It is the wealth transfer coming to you that has taken place in the unseen spirit realm! You must get it into the earth realm. It is money coming from drug dealers to you. It's those who have built big corporations off the backs of the poor and working class. It is in your hands right now, *"not by might, nor by power but by my spirit says the Lord"* (Zechariah 4:6).

"Hidden treasures" means unexpected income is coming through you, favor is coming through you, money is on its way through you in every imaginable means, including unclaimed funds, lost money, and lost wealth.

Debt cancellation and Wealth Acceleration!

Money will track you down!

I met with one of my spiritual sons outside the fellowship. He said, "Brother Charles, here's a gift for you. I just wanted to honor you as my spiritual father."

Money will chase you down when you are under the anointing!

> *For I was envious at the foolish, when I saw the prosperity of the wicked!*
>
> (Psalm 73:3)

David was concerned when he wrote this passage because He saw so many wicked people prospering. As you read this book, you probably know some folks who are not living a proper life–shacking up, lying and stealing, smoking dope, knocking old ladies in the head–yet they look like they are prospering. However, they are prospering through satanic or worldly anointing.

Have you ever been envious of someone who was wicked and yet was prospering? Verse 12 speaks further about these people:

> *Behold, these are the ungodly, who prosper in the world; they increase in riches.*

But, that's not the end of the story. Look what follows in verse 17 when David essentially says, "Yes, I was envious and discouraged..."

> *Until I went into the sanctuary of God; then I understood their end.*

When David entered into the presence of the Lord, he discovered that the wealth of the wicked was going to be transferred!

Surely thou didst set them in slippery places: thou casteth them down into destruction.

(Psalm 73:18)

Before the wicked die, all that money and wealth they possess is destined to flow into the hands of the righteous - you and me!

The Set Time—the Kairos time

There is a Kairos time zone established for the release of your money and your wealth anointing in the earth. Your impartation and manifestation has a set time.

There is a time zone of opportunity, of promise, of order and establishment, of completion and acceleration. I have a prophetic word for you concerning this time zone for your money release, your material release, your favor release.

Arise, shine; for the light is come, and the glory of the LORD is risen upon thee.

(Isaiah 60:1)

That word "glory" is not the glory presence of God here, but in this context it means "the wealth and honor" that God is wanting to place upon you.

Then thou shall see, and flow together, and thine heart shall fear, and be enlarged...

(Isaiah 60:5)

Imagine. God is saying that through the breath, the length, the height, and the depth of the anointing, you are going to be enlarged! Why?

...because the abundance of the sea shall be converted unto thee, the forces of the Gentiles shall come unto thee.

(Isaiah 60:5)

These forces, the wealth and the riches of the Gentiles, is ready to come upon you now! The time zone for your money and wealth is right now. Not tomorrow. Right now you have the abundance. It will come as you complete this book, as you go to work tomorrow. Look through the eyes of the spirit. Your money is not just coming, it is here! Act as though you have the money. Begin to look in your mail box for the new money.

> *But thou, O LORD, shalt endure for ever; and they remembrance unto all generations. Thou shalt arise, and have mercy upon Zion: for the time to favour her, yea, the set time, is come.*
> (Psalm 102: 12-13)

We are Zion, we are the *ekklesia*, we are the called out ones to be a blessing to others.

And here's the next part of this staggering revelation!

> *When the LORD shall build up Zion, He shall appear in His glory.*
> (Psalm 102:6)

You are Zion. The Lord wants to first build you up <u>before</u> He appears in His glory? God is not coming to a weak and financially strapped fellowship. God is looking for His righteous people to be holy, strong and rich to usher in His return!

> *Repent ye therefore and be converted that your sins may be blotted out for when the times of refreshing shall come from the presence of the Lord.*
> (Acts 3:19)

When is the time of refreshing? Right now.

"Refreshing" means "relief." The Lord is sending money relief right now.

Now, let us look at Galatians 4:4

> *But when the fullness of the time was come, God sent forth His Son, made of a woman, made under the law.*

This is the fullness of time!

We are not waiting on money and wealth to come, they are already here.

We are not waiting for a healing to come, healing is already here.

Joy is already here.

Faith is already here.

It's a NOW money zone, a NOW money season, a set money time. The best time to be healed is right NOW, not tomorrow.

God sent Christ the Anointed One, who died on the cross that you and I may be free from the curse of the law.

Rise up and walk.

Save now, I beseech thee, O LORD: O LORD, I beseech thee, send now prosperity.

(Psalm 118: 25)

"Lord, Your children are ready to receive Your prosperity now! Lord, we beseech You to prepare us to receive and walk in your prosperity now!"

I pray that as you read this book, God will release through you...

Now wealth.
Now divine influence and favor.
Now divine dreams and visions.
Now abundance.
Now joy.
Now healing.
Now deliverance.
Now exposure.
Now money.

Lord, send Your Church and Your children prosperity now!

CHAPTER SEVEN

Living in the Invisible

There are five realms of the spirit:

1. The Demonic Realm.
2. The Human Realm.
3. The Angelic Realm.
4. The Holy Spirit Realm.
   The realm of the Holy Spirit is where God dwells. It is the invisible, third heaven. The anointing comes from this realm (the third dimension of grace).
5. The Recreated Human Spirit Realm.
   This is the human spirit recreated by Christ in you.

Recreated human spirits are invisible, and the money anointing operates in the invisible realm, making it difficult for many Christians to grasp and apply that anointing in their own lives.

God is a spirit; and they that worship him must worship him in spirit and truth.

(John 4:24)

Our recreated human spirits are part of God and His Spirit. When we see each other, we see a reflection of God in the earth. We are not all that God is, but we are enough of what He is so we can achieve what God wants us to accomplish here on the earth.

And all things are of God, who hath reconciled us to himself by Jesus Christ...

(II Corinthians 4:18)

Since God operates in the invisible realm, we need to

stop focusing on things which can only be seen. Stop trying to understand stuff in the natural realm. "All things are of God," but He operates in the realm of the invisible.

Stop dwelling on your twisted body...it is not your real body. Focus on your invisible body. Stop looking at the tumor and start looking at where your body is going to end up—in the realm of the invisible, permanent and eternal.

If you are sick, start declaring, "That's not me! That's what I look like in the natural realm, but that is not my glorified body."

You want to lose weight?

Focus on the invisible, the realm of the spirit, and the weight will start falling off as your vision gets closer to the invisible.

Start seeing God on the throne with Jesus at the right hand of the Father. Start seeing yourself the way God sees you: healed, delivered, blessed, sanctified, joyful, and walking in His righteousness.

We are Products of the Unseen!

> *While we look not at the things which are seen, but at the things which are not seen: for the things which are seen are temporal: but the things which are not seen are eternal.*
>
> (II Corinthians 4:18)

The invisible part of you IS more than a conqueror. The invisible part of you IS destined to become wealthy in all the aspects of God. You CAN do *"all things through Christ"* who strengthens you (Philippians 4:13). Start to say, "As of today I declare an end to what I see. I will begin to have godly attitudes about myself and others, and I ask the Holy Spirit to teach me how to see and focus on the invisible things of God in my life."

152

Things <u>seen</u> are temporary, but things <u>not seen</u> are eternal. Start to stand in prayer to receive your...

- Unseen healing.
- Unseen health.
- Unseen money.
- Unseen deliverance.
- Unseen joy.
- Unseen peace.
- Unseen new homes.
- Unseen paid bills.
- Unseen exposure.

Begin to feel the spiritual force, the spiritual magnet around you.

Romans 1:20 says,

For the invisible things of him from the creation of the world are clearly seen, being understood by the things that are made, even his eternal power and Godhead; so that they are without excuse:

Your imagination is the program software for your invisible computer. You can either plug in a carnal software tape or one that blesses your spiritual imagination. We all need to decide which tape we will plug in, remembering that all our happiness, all of our joy, **all of our fulfillment comes from the unseen!**

One New Year's Eve when I was walking and praying with God for a full ninety minutes in the Spirit, thanking the Lord for the things He had given me and my family in the last year. In the midst of that spiritual time, He gave me a revelation that has changed my life. He told me, "You must live and walk in the unseen where all of My glory is."

We are products of the unseen! We were birthed from the invisible.

Who is the image of the invisible God, the firstborn of every creature:

(Colossians 1:15)

Who is the image of the invisible? God, the first born of every creature.

For by him all things were created, that are in heaven, and that are in the earth, visible and invisible, whether they be thrones, or dominions, or principalities, or powers: all things were created by him, and for him.

(Colossians 1:16)

The anointing is in the realm of the invisible, and your money is going to be received from the invisible. After you receive it in the invisible, it will manifest itself in the visible. This sounds really mystical but the invisible is a created realm of God. Your thoughts must be renewed in order to appreciate the invisible realm of the Holy Spirit.

One day I was looking over Cincinnati in the realm of the invisible and I saw a new heaven and a new earth with godly principalities, godly dominions, and godly thrones. All over the city I saw the glory, the presence of the Lord hovering.

Now unto the King eternal, immortal, invisible, the only wise God, be honour and glory for ever and ever. Amen.

(I Timothy 1:17)

Now look at Hebrews 11:27.

By faith, he forsook Egypt, not fearing the wrath of the king: for he endured, as seeing him who is invisible.

We are dealing with an invisible anointing!

So then faith cometh by hearing, and hearing by the Word of God.

(Romans 10:17)

Out of your heart flows the issues of life (Proverb 4:23). Out of your anointing flows all the issues you are trying to deal with in your life. Cancer. Tumors. Money.

Your children see you in the visible but they need to know that you also live in the invisible. At home, I speak in tongues as I walk the treadmill so my kids know that their Daddy lives in both the visible and invisible. It is important for them to see me worshiping God, hollering and screaming, seeking God in our home. They cannot learn how to stand in the presence of the Lord without learning how to manifest praise and worship to the King of Kings in the invisible.

Practice entering into the presence of the Lord. Begin to see the throne of God. See Jesus sitting on the throne with a crown around His head and the glory of the Lord upon Him. Be like the 24 elders, singing "Holy, holy Lord God almighty, who was and is to come."

Already Resurrected!

And hath raised us up together, and made us sit together in heavenly places in Christ Jesus:

That in the ages to come he might shew the exceeding riches of his grace in his kindness toward us through Christ Jesus.

(Ephesians 2:6-7)

Do you see it? You are not only going to be resurrected in the future, <u>you are already resurrected</u>!

The only resurrection left for you to experience is the uniting of your spirit, soul and body into an unseen, glorified body. But, the Bible says we have **already** been raised up together with Him!

You cannot have a resurrection unless you have already been dead. We died with Christ, and have been buried and resurrected with Him.

In the invisible...we are already resurrected! God has already allowed us to sit with Him in a heavenly place or a real state.

> *But let it be the hidden man of the heart, in that which is not corruptible, even the ornament of a meek and quiet spirit, which is in the sight of God of great price.*
>
> (1 Peter 3:4)

This hidden place is the dwelling place of the anointing!

God is appropriating Himself. Although He's in the invisible realm, He's appropriating Himself in us in the earthly realm through the visible.

We are the visible reflection of the invisible God. And, the invisible anointing we have within us is not corruptible.

> *Therefore I say unto you, What things soever ye desire when ye pray, believe that ye receive them, and ye shall have them.*
>
> (Mark 11:24)

See the "things you desire" first in your spirit, mind and imagination. Monitor what goes into your head. Monitor your thoughts moment by moment. Taking in the wrong desires (those that go against God's will) could set you back for days, months or even years by inputting wrong programming on your invisible computer.

Psalm 66:12 was given to me on October 23, 2002 in Marshall Texas, where my spiritual father, Randy Shankle, told the corporate body to turn to someone and prophesy to them. "Give them a word from the Lord," he said. Brother Jeff Arrington turned and prophesied this Scripture over me.

> *Thou hast caused men to ride over our heads; we went through fire and through water; but thou broughtest us out into a wealthy place.*
>
> (Psalm 66:12)

In war, many tell stories of enemy soldiers passing right over their heads while they were hidden down in the muddy trenches. They had to be quiet because if the enemy soldiers heard them, they would have been blown away. This prophetic Scripture describes the perils of symbolic fire and water we all face in life, similar to those of a real enemy attack. And, it provides prophetic hope for the future!

But He has brought us out of the fire and water and into a wealthy place!

How to Enter Your Wealthy Place

You enter your wealthy place when you enter the unseen realm. **When you seek God's face you create a wealthy place!** As you walk in the unseen realm with right thoughts, your wealth will automatically come and manifest itself visibly.

> *But let it be the hidden man of the heart, in that which is not corruptible, even the ornament of a meek and quiet spirit, which is in the sight of God a great price.*
> (I Peter 3:4)

The corruptible has put on incorruption. The mortal has put on immortality.

> *For this corruptible must put on incorruption, and this mortal must put on immortality.*
>
> *So when this corruptible shall have put on incorruption, and this mortal shall have put on immortality, then shall be brought to pass the saying that is written, Death is swallowed up in victory.*
> (1 Corinthians 15:53&54)

1 Corinthians 9:25 expands this concept by saying,

> *And every man that striveth for the mastery is temperate in all things. Now they do it to obtain a corruptible crown; but we an incorruptible.*

You and I wear incorruptible crowns, and we inherit the right to wealth and abundance.

> *Being born again, not of corruptible seed, but of an incorruptible, by the Word of God, which liveth and abideth for ever.*
>
> (1 Peter 1:23)

The incorruptible is in the realm of the invisible, and it is in the invisible that we shall live for eternity.

You release the money anointing in the realm of the spirit. Your wealth, health, and abundance are going to come in the realm of the spirit, through the anointing in the invisible, unseen realm. It will break loose all around you. You are going to suddenly come into it because you are so highly anointed. Enoch and Elijah were so anointed by God that they were spiritually translated and did not die a physical death. Don't you want to be anointed?

> *While we look not at the things which are seen, but at the things which are not seen: for the things which are seen are temporal; but the things which are not seen are eternal*
>
> (2 Corinthians 4:18)

If you look only at what you see, you will be disappointed. Learn to look at things not seen. The only way to see the "not seen" is to be trained on how to live in the realm of the spirit.

Start to see your wealth, your abundance, your healing, your prosperity in the spirit. Walk in the anointing, full of the glory of God!

The things which are seen are temporary!

Moments Away

In the natural realm, we live in a temporary state. Your situation is not going to remain like it is because soon you are going to experience change! Your breakthrough and release are on the way via the invisible realm.

God is giving you a new heart as you work in your old job. You will experience a new spouse in an old marriage.

Permanency is right round the corner, and it is called "eternal." Your spouse may be drinking beer now, but soon he or she will be drinking a new wine.

In the unseen realm your supernatural breakthrough is just a few moments away, so don't give up!

If you had given up, you wouldn't be reading this book today to receive the revelation of the money anointing.

If you had given up, you would not know in your spirit that...
   • Your super spiritual breakthrough.
   • Your super spiritual impartation.
   • Your super spiritual manifestation.
   • Your super spiritual miracle.
   • Your super spiritual money are all already here!

Receive the first fruits of the spirit, the anointing of the Lord.

> *And not only they, but ourselves, also, which have the first-fruits of the Spirit...*
>
> (Romans 8:23)

As His heir, as a son of God, you inherit the first fruits of the anointing. **Your initial money is coming to you in the spirit so you can sow your first fruits and begin to activate that which is in the invisible.**

You and I are sons of God, His first fruits in the earth. By way of Abraham, Isaac, and Jacob, we inherited their Shemen because we are the first fruits of Christ.

As you read this book, I believe the initial money anointing is entering into your atmosphere in the spirit right now. You and I are the first fruits of the earth, the carriers of the anointing. We do not carry disease, sickness or poverty, we are carriers of the anointing!

Your first fruits money is coming because of the anointing. Dr. Creflo Dollar said, "Your payday is on it's way." You will receive the prophets reward, your compensation for receiving the man of God.

Ezekiel 44:30 says,

And the first of all the first-fruits of all things, and every oblation of all, of every sort of your oblations, shall be the priest's; ye shall also give unto the priest the first of your dough, that he may cause the blessing to rest in thine house.

Oblation means "offering." Bring every offering to the priests, apostles, prophets, so they may release a blessing upon your house.

God is giving you power to establish the covenant of God so that you can help people be better off, and establish God's covenant. The priest needs money to proclaim the Gospel of the Kingdom and to help bring others out of poverty.

That is why you bring your first fruits offerings to the priest, and he then releases the blessing upon you. This is one way to release the blessings of God on you. It is not the only way.

Respect and honor the pastors, apostles and prophets, but get anointed yourself. I pray you do not have to depend on them for your blessings. Then you can turn around and be a big financial blessing to them.

In the Old Testament, the function spoken of here was called, "priest," and in the New Testament that same function would be called an "elder," or "apostle" or "prophet."

160

CHAPTER EIGHT

Act as Though You Have It!

By now I hope you are starting to declare something like this: "I am out of debt, and I have plenty of money to invest into others!" To release the money anointing you must first start to act as though you already have it because you are in a revelational time zone, an invisible zone. I don't like this statement, "Fake it until you make it." I say you either have the money anointing or you don't. The word "fake it" is a false representation. This anointing that I am talking about is real.

Do not look at things which are seen and temporary. Look for things which are permanent and eternal. If you have developed the ability to look into the realm of the spirit, you will be able to operate in the **revelational time zone**, spending time around the throne of God in the invisible, seeing what others are not able to see.

If we keep seeing the unseen realm, sooner or later it will manifest itself and end up in our hands. The wealth of the wicked will actually manifest over time and end up in our hands. And, money from the righteous will also come our way.

Visualize the Unseen

What you see in the invisible realm is what you will possess. So, when you claim the money anointing by faith, you are operating in the realm of the invisible. As you spend your time in the realm of the invisible, your attitude, your mind, your thoughts, and your emotions begin to change. As you visualize your wealth, your abundance, and your prosperity, you begin to receive that wealth. As you visualize how to handle money, and how to handle wealth, your mind and emotions are being renewed. Your attitudes about healing are going to be different as you spend time in the unseen, around the throne room of God. **Keep in mind one of the purposes of money is to help others have a better life on earth.** Zig Zigler said, "If you help enough other people to get what they want in life, enough other people will help you get what you want in life." Money for the sake of money is greed at its worst. Just having material money should not be your goal. Material money, in the hands of a person without character, is a bad thing.

Start visualizing in the unseen realm! Right now, in the visible, you have the ability to handle big money. But as you continue to spend time in the invisible, you will soon have the ability to manage millions of your own and others because you will be transformed. The goal is not to get a million dollars in the bank. **The goal must be to continue to circulate all monies to be a blessings to others, and the money will be returned to you.**

Act as though you already have it!

Visualize yourself as a son of God, with your pattern for life being Jesus Christ. As you do, you will become more and more like Him. Keep your imagine in the mirror of the unseen and eventually you will become like Him. Remember, the day is coming when we are going to have a glorified body.

Act as though you have it now: your money, your wealth, your material blessings, your healing. The release of the money anointing is being downloaded in a divine time zone, a span of time where you can see where others are not able to see.

Come into His tabernacle, the holy of holies, the realm of the invisible.

If you look at your spouse right now, it may discourage you. That is why it is important to see in the unseen realm.

162

See your spouse as new and transformed. See your children in the future as changed, shaken, tilted, broken, and developed in God, leading and ruling the nation!

The word "Shemen" refers to the Old Testament anointing that destroys the yolk. Today, we have an even better anointing through Christ the Anointed One. We have a triple anointing of Shemen (the God of the Old Testament) plus Christos (the God of the New Testament), which is the Father, the Son and the Holy Ghost - all three in one, a triple anointing in the Godhead. Then add one other anointing–the Rhema anointing, making it a quad-triple anointing. All of the expressions of God working on our behalf.

So start acting as though you have already received your money anointing in the revelational zone.

<u>Here's an absolute anointing truth:</u>

It is often said,

You will never have the anointing until you first see it!

And where are you going to see it?

Not in the first heaven, not here on earth or in the heavenly atmosphere where all the planes fly.

Not in the second heaven, where all the demons and evil spirits reside. Satan is the ruling prince and power of the air in the second heaven. He constantly is working on your mind. That is why you must constantly transform your mind through God's Word. Every time you say, "I am healed," Satan will say, "No you're not." Satan wants to bring you back into the visible realm, the realm of the natural eye using your bad thoughts against you.

Your anointing will come as you learn to live each day in the third heaven, the realm of the unseen, the invisible realm. You cannot believe it until you see it in the invisible realm.

You need to start being seated together with Him in heavenly places. You now have an open heaven backing you up. Go forward in the realm of the spirit.

I have decided to cut deals in the realm of the unseen. That is why I am able to talk about our new encampment, a $2 million Training and Prayer Center. Our fellowship first visualized it in the unseen, and in time they will actually see it come to pass right before their very eyes.

Initially when God birthed the vision for the encampment of the Apostolic Training Base in my spirit (the unseen), I did not poll the leaders of the church, trying to determine what they thought. Because I am a son of God, living in the **revelational time zone**, I started to look in the realm of the spirit and said, "We can have that Apostolic Training Base or Encampment. It belongs to us. In my Father's house there are many mansions. Lord, I take possession of those new buildings so our local fellowship can be a better blessing to others in the city and region."

I decided to live in the unseen realm and bask in His divine presence, coming before Him with thanksgiving, adoration, and honor.

Get into the unseen realm and constantly renew yourself in the Word of God every day.

God is a spirit and they that worship him may worship him in spirit and in truth.

(John 4:24)

The **manifestational time zone** is in the physical realm (your body), called the *Soma*. The transformational visualizations take place in the *Pneuma*, the Greek word for spirit. *Psyche* is the Greek word for soul where your thoughts, mind, will, and emotions reside.

Receive the End of Your Faith

What is the end of your faith?

You were finished first. God started and finished you all in the same hour, so He knows what your end is going to be.

Get out of the seen realm because it will mess you up. Every day you must live with the end in mind. Start to see the end of your money, the end of your wealth and abundance. By saying, "see the end" I mean "reaching the target" up front so we have it right now.

Receiving the end of your faith.

(1 Peter 1:9)

So, you can be a blessing to hundreds and thousands of people.

We cannot see our children the way they are now, we must see them at the end of who they are. What you see now in the natural is not really how they are going to turn out. (Someone reading this should say, "Praise the Lord!) See the end of your spouse, and live that end every day.

Here's a Divine Revelation:

God made the end before He made the beginning!

He made your end first, and now you must learn how to live that end. To reverse the beginning you must see your end, constantly striving toward the end, not the beginning. The beginning is the trial time, the suffering time, the stress time, the rehearsal time, the affliction time. You do not want to spend much time there...you want to see the end.

As you see the end...

The affliction does not hurt so much.

A cancer setback does not destroy your life. (My dear wife, Coleen Winburn, recovered from breast cancer.)

Kidney problems are just temporary.

165

As you see the end, you know you are not always going to be like this. Challenge and conflict does not matter because you are constantly seeing your end.

Live in your end, not your beginning. The beginning is a jump start to your present future.

> *Receiving the end of your faith, even the salvation of your souls.*
>
> (1 Peter 1:9)

Your end is wealth, abundance, prosperity, money, divine health, joy, peace, and righteousness, coming into the presence of God.

> *Searching what, or what manner of time the Spirit of Christ which was in them did signify, when it testified beforehand the sufferings of Christ, and the glory that should follow.*
>
> (1 Peter 1:11)

You must constantly search for the manner of time when the Spirit of Christ, the Anointed One, will manifest itself.

Satan is NOT in Control

God is in control of heaven, but Satan is not in control of this earth. We are in control of the earth through ruling and reigning. There is only one power and that's the power of God. There are not two powers. Satan is ruling from the second heaven, trying to snatch you out of the revelational time zone. He essentially says, "I am going to try to snatch the message of the transformational time zone out of your mind by the time you go to bed tonight. Whatever you are doing–be it cooking or eating–I will try and snatch the transformational teaching out of your mind." (Transformation teaching is that teaching which changes your mind or thoughts.)

Satan is operating out of the second heaven, so He cannot control you on earth. We must recapture the earth by ruling and reigning now. The earth is the Lord's.

People who are sick all the time, poor all the time, broke all the time, want to blame God. But they are in their current conditions because they want to be in those conditions. Because of thoughts, they think Satan has power over them. There is only one power and that is God.

God controls heaven. You are destined to rule and reign the earth through the power of Jesus Christ. But, God will not control and guide you unless you give Him permission through your mind or thoughts.

> *The LORD God of your fathers make you a thousand times so many more as ye are, and bless you, as he hath promised you!*
>
> (Deuteronomy 1:11)

You are healed according to the unseen realm of faith as you walk the end out every day. If you keep seeing the invisible long enough, you will begin to change. See yourself healed, see yourself as financially matured in the things of God. Your end is your healing, your deliverance, your prosperity, your wealth.

You need your beginning to get to your end.

It is your time to live in abundance, to live the end of your prayers, to live the end of your fasting, to live the end of your sowing money.

Someone would call visualizing the unseen as a "new age" teaching. But the truth is we live in the invisible realm every day. No person can see themselves. They only see their physical and natural self in a mirror. No one has seen God, but we believe in Him any way. In the physical realm humans are the reflections and expressions of God in the Earth.

> *Be not deceived; God is not mocked: for whatsoever a man soweth, that shall he also reap.*
>
> (Galatians 6:7)

Do not give up. Help is on the way.

Hear, ye children, the instruction of a father, and attend to know understanding.

(Proverbs 4:1)

If I had to choose between wisdom and money, I would choose wisdom any day because money is flexible. Money on the material level comes and goes. I spend hundreds of hours studying. I have probably spent a thousand hours in study to receive this key revelation on how to release the money anointing through tapes, videos by such men as Mike Murdock, John Avanzini, Dr. Creflo Dollar, Leroy Thompson, Kenneth Copeland, and many others. Why did I do this? Because I want to be a real financial blessing to others. The more I became saturated with the Word of God, the more I broke loose in the spirit. The more I break loose in "Shemen," the more I break loose in "Christos."

While the earth remaineth, seedtime and harvest, and cold and heart, and summer and winter, and day and night shall not cease.

(Genesis 8:22)

Without an impartation on how to release the money anointing, you will be destined to spending your life undermining others, playing the lottery and bingo, and doing illegal, immoral, unethical things such as cheating on your income tax, and more. This is culture running after material money.

Trust God as Your Source

Call on heaven to provide everything you need. Constantly prepare yourself through fasting and prayer, seeking the Lord to release the Shemen and the Christos anointing.

Some people live their lives in the wrong places, and keep on doing what they have always done. **You will**

never be broke another day in your life once you decide you are going to solve the right people problems, such as going into business. Maybe someone needs a computer technician. Begin to take the computer courses you need.

Start working on solving the right problem and you will never be broke.

You will become mean and mad at other people if you decide that they are going to be your source.

Wives, your husband is not your source. When a wife sees her man as her source, according to Mike Murdock, and he fails to give her money, she will turn on that man, embarrassing him, putting him down because she thinks the man owes her. The Bible says, "Owe no man" but to love.

God is our source. God can use people like us to pass through money, but we must always remember that our money comes from God.

Trust God to bring you money in unexpected places and dimensions with unexpected people!

Learn to invest so your life can be transformed.

Study this book many times. It functions like a university of money.

God has His anointing seed in you. You are becoming what God has planted in you, so start living in the end of your faith, not the beginning.

You are the Seed of God in the Earth

For God so loved the world, that he gave his only begotten Son, that whosoever believeth in him should not perish, but have everlasting life.

(John 3:36)

There are things planted in you such as visions, dreams, ideas, creativity, and witty inventions. **You are much more than what you see, and what others see in you.** As I grew up, others told me, "Charlie Winburn, you will never amount to anything." They saw me in the seen realm, but God, in the unseen realm, said "Greater is He that is in me than he that is in the world."

Some think the tree is the fruit, but the fruit is really the seed.

God started with a seed anointing. You were birthed because of a seed. My father and mother planted the seed of Charlie Winburn. Your goal is to constantly get out of your beginnings to stay focused on your end.

And he shall be like a tree planted by the rivers of water, that bringeth forth his fruit in his season; his leaf also shall not wither; and whatsoever he doeth shall prosper.

(Psalm 1:3)

You are like a tree planted by the rivers of water. According to the Bible, in a season your leaf shall not wither. Whatever you do, you need to be prospering in your love life, with your children, on the job.

Water your seed garden so it will bear fruit.

If you had more money, you could help make other people's lives better (unless you are selfish). When I get additional money, everybody around me prospers. So, one of the purposes of money is to make others better off in the earth, to give to others to establish the covenant of God in the earth.

There is No Shortage!

That is a lie from the devil and people.

There is no scarcity! There is surplus!

The universe is an abundant, wealthy territory. The only lack, the only shortage is in your mind. The money anointing always releases your original financial seed. Your initial seed is coming. Take that initial seed and put it back into the Kingdom, the local fellowship, or apostolic work or Christian television.

> *Verily, verily I say unto you, whosoever shall say unto this mountain, mountain be thou removed and be thou cast in the sea and shall not doubt in his heart but shall believe those things which he has said they shall come to pass.*
>
> (Mark 11:23)

Speak with God's eternal purpose. Never say that you are poor unless you want to be.

Even when I feel a sickness coming on me, I will never communicate it. The moment you say something about sickness, evil spirits, launched in the second heavens, come and stir up that which you speak. Your thoughts begin to attract that which is evil.

Stop communicating how you feel because your feelings are not faith! Someone said, "you better manage your feelings before they manage you."

The Bible says, *"That which is not of faith is sin"* (Romans 14:23). If you do not want to be poor, stop talking poor. Learn to walk in joy, no matter what circumstances you are facing. Let your life be built solely upon Jesus Christ and His righteousness.

Why Money is Important

Money gives you freedom...you are free to do more, to spend more time with your family, to exercise, to go out of town on vacation, and to be a blessing to others.

When you receive divine health, healing and money, you become a dangerous person because you will have the power to tread on serpents and scorpions.

171

Someone said, "Your greatest wealth is you!"

When you receive divine health, healing, prosperity, the super spiritual, the Shemen anointing, and the Christos anointing, and the pneuma anointing, and the Rhema anointing, working within you, then you become your greatest wealth.

YOU ARE THE WEALTH OF GOD!

You are wealthy in your relationships, in your transformed mind, wealthy with a manifestation of the wisdom of God.

You are your greatest wealth.

The Wealth of God

You are the resources, the invaluable possessions and riches of God in the Earth. ShunDrawn A. Thomas in his book, Start Planting, states, "Whether you admit it or not, money matters." Those who say "money doesn't really matter" to them have either one of two problems (or both):

1.   They are liars; or
2.   They have false humility.

Thomas further states, "It's not what you know, it's who you know."

Most people, in the natural realm, believe it is who you know and have relationship with that really counts. This may be true in some cases. However, from a spiritual perspective, it is really who you know that will make you wealthy, give you favor, joy, peace and righteousness in the Holy Ghost. If you know and have a relationship with the following, you will go places in heaven and earth through the Godhead:

1.   God in creation (Shemen Anointing).
2.   Christ in Redemption (Christos Anointing).

3. Holy Spirit in Truth (Pneuma Anointing).
4. The Word (the Rhema Anointing).

God has already done all He is going to do until Jesus comes back. Of course, God is always there, and we can run to Him for revelation and wisdom. After He is finished touching you with Shemen, Christos, Pnuema and Rhema. He is going to say, "Read your Bible and go do what you are suppose to do. You are your greatest wealth."

Choose life or death.

You have a free choice to do what you want to do. But, if you do not obey God and live right, doing what you need to do, then He will not dwell with you in peace.

CHAPTER NINE

The Force of Creative Imagination

We have been made in the image of God: He has an imagination, and we have an imagination. We need to see the things that God has for us through our imagination, the invisible realm. It is a great force that God has given us to see things in the unseen realm. Your imagination is a gateway to the prophetic realm. When we see each other, we are pretty close to seeing how God looks in the natural.

During my senior year in high school, my teacher told me to go to a technical college because he felt I would not do well in a university (yet I graduated in the middle of my high school class). In 1973, using the principle of "imagining myself" graduating from the University of Cincinnati, I graduated with a 3.5 average in the upper third of my class! I made the Dean's list several times. In 1975, I used the principles of creative imagination and ended up with a full scholarship, graduating with a 3.8 average from graduate school with a master's degree in education from the University of Cincinnati.

The power of creative imagination, coupled with the anointing of God, will allow you to accomplish much in the earth. Get busy developing your imagination in the Word of God.

God had a great imagination when He made you. Have you looked in the mirror lately? Just think, you are the creation of God's imagination. When you see yourself, you see how God looks.

I also used creative imagination when I was placed in foster homes. I saw myself no longer on welfare, but prosperous, having more than enough abundance to be a blessing to others in the earth. I don't support New Age philosophy. The force of creative imagination is from the "God Age," not "New Age." The Bible says "there is nothing new under the sun." In the beginning was God, period. Develop your imagination through the anointing and the Word.

The Anointed Imagination

When the anointing smears your mind, you will be able to see what you believe before it happens, because your mind is renewed.

> *I beseech you therefore, brethren, by the mercies of God, that ye present your bodies a living sacrifice, holy, acceptable unto God, which is your reasonable service. And be not conformed to this world: but be ye transformed by the renewing of your mind, that ye may prove what is that good, and acceptable, and perfect, will of God.*
>
> (Romans 12:1-2)

You are the imagination of God to call into existence your unseen desires.

> *And God said, Let us make man in our image, after our likeness: and let them have dominion over the fish of the sea, and over the fowl of the air, and over the cattle, and over all the earth. So God created man in his own image, in the image of God created he him; male and female created he them.*
>
> (Genesis 1:26-27)

* See yourself as the wealth of God!
* See yourself blessing people with money, wealth and abundance!
* See yourself president of a real estate company.
* See yourself owning that $50 million business.
* See yourself as the best stock and money investor.

• See yourself selling a $100 million insurance policy.

The anointing will help you to see before you actually possess it or before it is physically manifested. The anointing will help you to concentrate so you will be able to see in the realm of the unseen. The anointing will teach you how to see, and help you creatively visualize your future. The anointing will train you how to manifest money, wealth, abundance, and materials so you can be a blessing to others.

The anointing will help you breakthrough and walk in an open heaven so you can achieve your desires in the earth. The anointing will take you into spiritual places where there are no boundaries or limitations, causing you to speak what is in your heart.

O generation of vipers, how can ye, being evil, speak good things? For out of the abundance of the heart the mouth speaketh.

(Matt. 12:34)

The anointing will change your thinking.

Now unto him that is able to do exceeding abundantly above all that we ask or think, according to the power that worketh in us...

(Eph. 3:20)

Two Personal Experiences

Through the years I have used my anointed imagination in many different ways to obtain money and strategic influence. Here's two examples.

In 1993, I was told that I could not win a seat on the Cincinnati City Council, and would not be able to raise the money to win because I was a first-time candidate, and a Republican in a Democratic city. But I saw myself in the unseen realm with one of those nine powerful seats on Cincinnati City Council. I also saw myself receiving money from many people that I didn't even know, giving me money to support my financial campaign. A few weeks before Election Day, my election finance report was given to the media disclosing that I had broken all fund raising records for a city council race, raising over $308,000, the largest amount ever raised in the history of Cincinnati for a city council race. I served three and a half terms on the Cincinnati City Council, raising over $1 million during that period.

I left a major denomination in 1986 and planted an apostolic work in Cincinnati after building a new church facility for that denomination. I started all over again. I used my anointed imagination and began to creatively imagine, in the unseen realm, purchasing real estate to build a new facility when I had no money in the bank. In 1987, we purchased land, built a new geodesic dome, and paid off the entire debt in two years. To date, this prime five-acre city estate is called "the Encampment"–the Church in College Hill, and is worth millions of dollars.

My Anointed Imagination Keeps On Working

Since I was 16 years old, I have always had a desire to attend a presidential convention. While my peers were out playing, I was in the house watching the presidential conventions. I saw myself at a presidential convention representing the state of Ohio. For years I would have spiritual flashbacks of the presidential conventions in my mind. Thirty-six years later, I still kept seeing myself at a political convention. It finally happened! I was at the National Republican Convention from Ohio when George Bush was nominated for the President of the United States of America. Governor Bob Taft of Ohio, a dynamic and wonderful governor, nominated me as an Ohio statewide alternate/delegate to the Republican Convention to nominate the next president of the United States in Philadelphia, Pennsylvania. That year George Bush became president of the United States of America.

God gives imagination to you. See it before you have it. Faith and anointing bring you into the unseen realm.

By October 2003, I had the opportunity to meet President George Bush twice. The first time I met him was when he was governor of Texas and came to Cincinnati to visit. The Second time was when Carl Lindner, Sr. invited my wife, Coleen and me to join the President for a reception at his son, Carl Lindner III's, home, in Indian Hills, Ohio, a very wealthy city. (I dedicated this book to Carl Lindner, Sr.).

Self-Talk and the Anointing

As you walk in the anointing, there will be no need to focus on self. Self-talk is what you say to yourself when no one is looking. The majority of people I know consistently say things to themselves that negatively undermine what little anointing they have, as well as their creative imagination. They are constantly feeding themselves with unbelief, doubt, and negative confessions.

Negative self-talk can sabotage your goals and visions! Negative self-talk is a whisper to yourself that you are not really what you display to others.

There is positive self-talk and negative self-talk. Positive self-talk is communicating to yourself what the Word of God has to say about you. The Word says that you are the righteousness of God. Negative self-talk says "I am not fully sure that the Word applies to me."

The Bible says, "Greater is He that is in me than he that is in the world." Negative self-talk says "I am not really that great." When you spend time in deep prayer and the Word of God, it will help you wash away negative self-talk.

Self-talk involves the process of programming or reprogramming. When you program your mind, moment by moment, with negative things about you or others, you create an image of your own world and you begin to walk out that destiny of negativity.

This is called the Law of Draw.

You will draw negative thoughts to you, and those thoughts will be manifested through other people. *You decide* if you want good or bad in your life. Whatever you think, you will surely get.

You must monitor what you say to yourself, moment by moment, and day by day. "As a man/woman thinketh in his/her heart, so is he/she."

What you keep saying to yourself, eventually you will become. If you talk to yourself about being sick, poor, and broke, you will become it.

We must obey the Word of God, and do what it states:

Whatsoever things are true, whatsoever things are honest, whatsoever things are just, whatsoever things are pure, whatsoever things are lovely, whatsoever things are of good report; think on these things.

(Philippians 4:8)

I believe this scripture is God's blueprint for programming your self-talk from a negative to a positive perspective. Bring an end to negative self-talk in your life, and begin to run after the anointing and presence of God.

I am convinced that most sicknesses are due to negative self-talk. You can talk yourself into poverty and sickness. I am not talking about promoting your ego or super soul, I am talking about getting rid of your stinking thinking. Negative self-talk can lead to pain, depression, oppression, obsession, and a host of other destructive things. Reprogram your self-talk with the Word of God and you will be on your way to receiving the explosion of the anointing of God.

Remember, no one can stop what God really has for you.

You shall have what you say.

(Mark 11:23)

The Oil (Wealth) of God

When the money anointing is upon you, it will work anywhere, any place.

Recently I gave some money to a man of God in Sharonsville. The church was packed that day. Upon releasing money to this man of God in the pulpit, people in the building got up and started coming forward, emptying their wallets to bless him. This pastor had cried out to God for years asking, "Lord, when is my turn going to come?" God used my presence and giving that day to give the preacher hope, to help improve his life, and to inspire others to give. These people needed the oil of the anointing.

The pastor cried for fifteen minutes that day. Money came to him from everywhere. He suddenly had money given to him spontaneously and unexpectedly.

One of the purposes of money is to make other people's lives prosper.

And you shall remember the Lord your God, for it is He who gives you power to get wealth, that he may establish His covenant which He swore to your fathers, as it is this day.

(Deuteronomy 8:18)

We need to help people become financially stable. Many people need someone to work with them financially until they are able to get where they need to be.

Like this pastor's experience, as you read this book, I believe you are going to be a new person, no longer stuck and stagnate.

This is your hour and your day!

Receiving the Anointing

The world accepts God's principles of money, abundance, and prosperity, but they reject Christ and His anointing. Their rejection proves that you can actually get money, wealth, and abundance without having the Anointed One and His anointing. You can have material money without God. You can have only spiritual money with God through the anointing. The children of darkness are frequently many times wiser than the children of light.

On the other hand, the Church accepts Christ, the Anointed One. This God-given anointing can unlock everything you need from spiritual wealth to financial wealth, from material wealth to physical wealth. It can unlock everything you need because Christ has anointed you.

Imagine what you can do by having Christ the Anointed One **AND** His anointing!

The moment someone in the world receives the Lord, they receive that special anointing from Christ.

There are those who are poor in spirit, lacking in their soul and body; they do not know that they have the wealth of God. They are not poor because they are Christians, but because they have rejected God's biblical principles.

Have you rejected the principles of money because you feel it is holy to be poor or broke? Just imagine what would come your way if you accept the principles of wealth, prosperity and money! Believe you are putting your hands on it. It may be coming in a small way, a large way, a phenomenal way, or an expected, or unexpected way.

How To Receive God's Principles

Say to yourself, "My time has come! This is my due season. I am coming out of debt and will have more than enough." You must change your negative thoughts on money.

If you are sitting in a fellowship where they do not teach and preach about this, all you will have is good messages, good phraseology, good oratorical abilities, but your life will never change. You need to have the Word of God, the transformation, the manifestation of God being preached and imparted.

With more money comes more freedom to do powerful things for the Kingdom of God.

There is more to invest into the lives of others.

There is more time to enjoy your children and your wife, your friends and relatives.

You have the spiritual freedom to worship God in the beauty of His holiness.

When you have money, you can also have divine health! When you have divine health, you do not need to be healed because there is no need for healing with divine health. Consequently, there is no need to ask for it because you have it!

The Wealth of God is Yours!

You are the wealth of God. Do not try to become wealthy. You already are because you have the God-Shemen anointing! God anointed all the men and women in the Old Testament with Shemen, beginning with Abraham, Isaac and Jacob. When the anointing fell on these three men, they began to live the abundant life.

When you get this oil of God on you, this Shemen, you will walk in health and prosperity. You will acquire houses, land and cattle on a million hills! You are the generational wealth of God.

Desire this oil that wakes you up at night, that causes

you to shout and dance, that gives you joy, peace and righteousness in the Holy Ghost. Ask for that oil that makes you preach, prophesy, and makes you wealthy and abundant.

Do you want that oil on you?

Receive this level of revelation concerning the Shemen and the ability to apply the God-anointing.

It shall come to pass in that day that his burden will be taken away from your shoulder, and his yoke from your neck, and the yoke will be destroyed because of the anointing oil.

(Isaiah10:27)

The anointing destroys the yoke. The Shemen obliterates the yoke of the debt, releasing your money, wealth, prosperity and abundance. It will make you whole in body, soul and spirit.

Let the oil of God get all over you! Bask in it. Tell yourself, "I am the wealth of God because I have the oil of God all over me. I have God dwelling in me."

Our deity is invisible and our humanity is visible. Our deity is invisible because no one can see God in us, but nevertheless He does reside within us. His deity brings us into our spiritual wealth and takes resident in us. Therefore, we are the wealth of God and His resources in the earth.

He is invisible, yet because we are visible, we are His visible wealth in this life.

You Are the Wealth of God

You are the wealth of God. Remember, you are not trying to get wealthy, you already are!

Nicodemus said to Him, "How can a man be born

when he is old? Can he enter a second time into his mother's womb and be born?

(John 3:4)

Nicodemus needed to rid himself of old thought patterns and conceptions. So too, you need to discard old thought patterns regarding money, healing, and beliefs which tell you that prosperity is not God's will.

By praying in the spirit, you already are in the invisible realm because part of you is invisible, part of you is deity. All that you need is in the invisible realm.

Get rid of your old traditions about money:

"I am poor."
"I am broke."
"I'll never have much."
Your life must be God-purposed!
When you speak, use a God-purposed vocabulary.

For assuredly, I say to you, whoever says to this mountain, 'Be removed and be cast into the sea,' and does not doubt in his heart, but believes that those things he says will come to pass, he will have whatever he says.

(Mark 11:23)

If you say "I am broke," "I am poverty-stricken," or "I am coming down with a cold," you will reap what you sow. You will have what you say. Mark 11:23 tells us those things will come to pass.

The Forces of Men and Angels

There are two forces working on your behalf on a 24-hour a day basis to help you get your financial wealth; men and angels.

God has people working on the earth for Him right now that He has talked to from the throne.

He turns to Jesus, dials up a number on the right hand of the Father and says, "Jesus, I want You to take care of someone on the earth. Go and give them wealth and abundance."

Then Jesus turns around and gives that message to the angels, and the angels of the Lord come down and deliver His message.

You have angels working on your behalf! They are bringing your deliverance and your money. They are helping you with your business so you can help establish the covenant of God here in the earth, proclaiming the Gospel of the Kingdom.

Because God has others working on your behalf, it is important that you have the anointing which will give you the wisdom and discernment regarding whom to trust. When you get the wisdom of that anointing, the Shemen and the Christos will direct you in knowing how to select your partnerships and associations.

You must constantly separate yourself from what is carnal. Cut carnal people out of your life in order to maintain your anointing and wisdom in God.

Acts 12:7 and Psalm 34:7 are examples of God using angels to intercede on behalf of men. Psalm 91 says:

He who dwells in the secret place of the Most High shall abide under the shadow of the Almighty.

I believe some of those shadows are angels of the Lord.

I believe there are angels coming for your words, coming for your thoughts! If you speak words of life such as "Greater is He that is in me," then He is coming to make those words a reality in your life. He wants you to be able to have it, touch it and see it (see Galatians 3:18-19 and Daniel 10:12).

If you believe there are angels of the Lord coming for your godly words, then it follows that there are demons and evil spirits coming for all your ungodly, negative words. They are looking for you. When you say, "I am sick," the demons rush to release more sickness. When you say, "I am poor," the evil spirits will do everything they can to bring you more poverty. When you say, "My marriage is no good," they will try to rock your marriage and tear it to shreds.

There are demons coming for your words, but you determine, by your choices, to give them power. There is only one real power in the universe and that is God.

What you speak is the sum total of who you are. If you are sick, you have helped to create that atmosphere. If you are prosperous, you have brought it on yourself because you are the wealth of God.

Who is Working for You?

If you own a business and you are working five or ten hours a day, you do not have a business, you have a job, and it will wear you out.

Wealthy people do not work for money, they allow money to work for them and through them.

Money is power. Even the drug dealers know more about entrepreneurship than some in the Body of Christ. They reject Christ, but they have adopted His principles. The business owner must change the paradigm of his business.

My children own their own businesses. Charlene has a typing business. I am her only client. Joseph has a money machine business. We bought him a little machine that counts money. I am his only client. He takes all of my coins and processes them through his machine. But the day is coming when they must change that business paradigm to grow a business. They cannot run a business with only one client.

I believe the only reason you should have a job is to use it as the foundation to start a business, to be a blessing to someone else, or to leverage the job to generate more money for investments. The job is really your seed money for investments into the work of God and to promote other investment opportunities for you and your family. If you have chosen a job to be your permanent place to accumulate money, that is just fine. However, turn that employment into a workplace and a marketplace for ministry.

The world teaches us to work hard and obtain a college degree. But frankly, I know many stupid people who have obtained college degrees. Many are in debt and on the verge of bankruptcy.

If you go to college, go with the intent of owning your own business. Otherwise, all you will be doing is chasing bonuses and negotiating for your wealth. I have three earned degrees so I am not knocking degrees and education.

When you own your own business, you create wealth. Learn how money works!

Hosea 4:6 says,

My people are destroyed for lack of knowledge.

Become familiar with the literary language of finances, and understand how it works.

For example, a house is not an asset. If you owe money on it, it is a liability. Yet we have been taught that a house is an asset because of the equity we store up. Until that house is paid for in full, it is a liability. Liability is fine if you can leverage that house to create greater revenue or income.

Create assets and learn how to create and make money work for you.

One of the quickest ways to cut your expenses and get out of debt is to reinvest your money in the Kingdom of God.

Destroy any credit cards in your possession. The only people who should have credit cards are people who have money. If you do not have the finances to pay for your credit cards on a timely basis, you are fooling yourself if there is no revenue to back it up!

Stop living in fear of not having enough. Stop accepting the lie that your current job offers you "security."

The only thing you should be working on is the vision of God. When you work on the vision of God, all that other stuff will take care of itself.

If you do all the work in your painting business by yourself, you do not have a business, you have a job. If you are working eight hours a day, you do not own a business, it owns you. A job is fine if you can leverage your money to increase revenue streams. Again a job is your seed money for investing into the kingdom. If all you are doing is paying the rent or the mortgage and buying groceries with your job, you are not going to be a great blessing to others.

Stop living in greed and fear. Kill the greed in you to make money, and kill the fear of losing the money. Make and circulate money because you want to advance the Kingdom of God.

It is understandable if you start off working eight or nine hours a day, but eventually you should be able to accumulate enough money to start a business. While working your eight-hour job, you can develop your business on the side. Eventually, your business will grow and you will have enough money to pay your salary and leave your job.

Most people work their jobs to create false security and insurance, and get stuck in that process. "If I just stay another ten years, I'm eligible for retirement." After retirement, the home is still not paid off, taxes and utilities have gone up, and the little retirement check simply cannot meet the monthly expenses.

Eradicate Fear

Discover the power of handling money, and do it without fear. Creating abundance should be fun, not stressful. **Be motivated by the anointing and not by the money.**

Your greatest competitor is yourself.

The fear of competition will only work against you, creating fear, heart palpitations, bipolarization, schizophrenia, and depression.

Eradicate fear so it won't control your life. Stop being afraid to leave your job and put money aside for a business. Stop waiting for retirement and death. It is time to live and declare the works of the Lord.

Fear not little children because it is your father's good pleasure to give you the kingdom of God.

(Luke 12:32)

If your heart is tender and innocent, it is your Father's HEART to give you the Kingdom. The Bible compares the Kingdom of God to a seed; when it grows, it expands. The Word of God is the sperma of God! The seed. When you receive the seed of God, it will bring about reproduction.

It is God's good pleasure to give you the Kingdom.

One reason you should have a job is for the purpose of starting a business. Or, leverage that money to generate new money so you can be a blessing to others.

Once you start your business, train someone up in that business to do your job. As time goes on, have several businesses at the same time. Develop trusted people to work for you and produce profits, creating your wealth so you can bless others.

Supervise your own workforce.

The Kingdom of God should be running the businesses,

and the world should be working for us. Get them sanctified, saved, and employed.

There is no fear in love. The Bible declares that there is no fear in God, only love.

If you are living in fear on your job and in your house, you cannot find rest. You will not be able to even enjoy the money you have because you are riddled with fear.

There is no fear in love; but perfect love casts out fear, because fear involves torment. But he who fears has not been made perfect in love.

(1 John 4:18)

Many millionaires who have made their money without God live in fear. They have ulcer problems, kidney problems, lung problems, and more.

But perfect love...the agape love of God, casts out all fear. Therefore, when we seek first the Kingdom of God and search for Him with all of our heart, soul and mind, the fear will always leave.

The Greek word for "fear" is phobia, which means "alarm." Have you ever seen people who are alarmed? They are frightened by their finances, their relationships, by most things in life.

I believe that most of our emotional and psychiatric problems, as well as our body's chemistry being thrown off, is due to the large amounts of adrenaline secreted by our bodies when we operate in fear. Hormones fall out of alignment, resulting in many mental and physical conditions.

Fear Torments

"Torment" means "the application of punishment." We should not punish our children, we should correct them.

If you punish your child, you create fear in them. Correction brings about the God kind of fear. Terror should never be struck into a child.

Negative fear in the Body of Christ dwells in those who are afraid to leave their secure jobs and venture out into owning their own businesses or investing their money into the Kingdom of God. If you cannot leave the job, try to form a part-time business so that you can create other revenue streams.

For you did not receive the spirit of bondage again to fear, but you received the Spirit of adoption by whom we cry out, "Abba, Father."

(Romans 8:15)

You have been adopted by your Heavenly Father, and He has given you the anointing, the Shemen, the Christos, Christ the Anointed One. When He adopted you, He anointed you!

I pray the Lord will help you eradicate fear from your life. Change your thoughts and the fear will leave.

There is no fear in love; but perfect love casts out fear, because fear involves torment. But he who fears has not been made perfect in love.

(1 John 4:18)

With Christ in your life, you can cast out all fear because in Him it is impossible to fail.

I can do all things through Christ who strengthens me.

(Philippians 4:13)

**You have the wealth of God
because
You have the God of wealth!**

Bless the Rich and Wealthy

*The rich and the poor have this in common, the
LORD is maker of them all.*

(Proverbs 22:2)

Don't curse the rich; bless them. If you bash the rich, you
will never become rich to the point where you will be able to
bless others. Cursing the rich comes from envy and jealousy
because you lack and want.

The Bible even tells us to bless those who despitefully
use you. The rich should not receive any less honor or
blessings because they are rich. The rich, especially in the
Body of Christ, should become liberal in their financial
giving and be a blessing to the apostolic work.

*For everyone to whom much is given, from him much
will be required;*

(Luke 12:48)

Everyone must receive the release of the money
anointing so that they can financially give on a large scale
in the "ministry of liberality." According to Dr. Dale M.
Sides, in his book The Ministry of Liberality, he states that
"the ministry of liberality, or the gift of giving, is an ability
given by God that enables certain people to make an
abundance of money."

A surplus of money is a good thing.

*Having then gifts differing according to the grace
that is given to us, whether prophecy, let us prophesy
according to the proportion of faith; Or ministry, let
us wait on our ministering: or he that teacheth, on
teaching; Or he that exhorteth, on exhortation: he
that giveth, let him do it with simplicity; he that
ruleth, with diligence; he that sheweth mercy, with
cheerfulness.*

(Romans 12:6-8)

One of the major purposes of money is to give it away and not just save or hoard it for your future. The purpose of the rich is to be a financial blessing to the apostolic Kingdom marketplace and the corporate Church.

Dr. Dale M. Sides illustrates the wrong use of money through Luke 12:17-19:

And he thought within himself, saying, What shall I do, because I have no room where to bestow my fruits? And he said, This will I do: I will pull down my barns, and build greater; and there will I bestow all my fruits and my goods. And I will say to my soul, Soul, thou hast much goods laid up for many years; take thine ease, eat, drink, and be merry.

Dr. Sides asks, "Whose money is it anyway?" Does it belong to the account of the rich man whose lands yielded plenty? Instead of giving that with which the Lord had blessed him, the rich man decided to save it and have plenty for the years to come. The fallacy in that way of thinking is to assume that those years are guaranteed. "Not so!" states Dr. Sides.

Charge them that are rich in this world, that they be not highminded, nor trust in uncertain riches, but in the living God, who giveth us richly all things to enjoy; That they do good, that they be rich in good works, ready to distribute, willing to communicate; Laying up in store for themselves a good foundation against the time to come, that they may lay hold on eternal life.

(I Timothy 6:17-19)

You don't have the right to curse someone and ask God to send them to heaven or hell. Stop cursing the rich because you personally lack in finances or materials. Go before the Lord and ask Him to give you the release of the anointing so that you can create money and attract money so you will have enough to give away.

Bless the rich! Bless the rich! Bless the rich!

Releasing the Money Anointing is the apostolic or "sending forth" of God's anointing upon you so you can go forth in the earth with money and be a blessing to others in the earth.

Where Are Your Treasures?

> *Do not lay up for yourselves treasures on earth, where moth and rust destroy and where thieves break in and steal; but lay up for yourselves treasures in heaven, where neither moth nor rust destroys and where thieves do not break in and steal.*
>
> (Matthew 6:19-21)

Releasing the Money Anointing is focused on laying up treasures in heaven, living in the realm of the spirit. For example, everything you need, you first get it in the realm of the spirit. In the spirit you first receive healing, divine health, deliverance, money, materials, revelation, transformation, insight, change, strategies and wisdom.

And there is a paradox to the anointing and living in the realm of the spirit. Although you live in the natural realm, you also live in the realm of the spirit, where the anointing is birthed.

Now is the time for you to lay up treasures that will positively impact this apostolic age. *"For where your treasure is, there your heart will be also"* (Luke 12:31-34). Your treasure and your heart are in the realm of the spirit, and the anointing of God.

The anointing is your treasure! Living in the realm of the spirit is your treasure in an earthen, anointed vessel.

There is nothing wrong with being rich as long as your wealth does not rule or possess you. God loves both the rich and the poor.

The rich and poor meet together: the LORD is the maker of them all.

(Proverbs 22:2)

If you desire to see rich people go to hell, then you must include in that group such Biblical people as Joseph, Abraham, Isaac, Jacob, David, Solomon, Joseph of Arimathea and Zacchaeus. Each of these people were rich with money or materials. If you don't want to be rich or wealthy, then at least be rich in faith, promoting love for all people.

CHAPTER TEN

Amazing Biblical
Truths About Money

And I John saw the holy city New Jerusalem coming down from God out of heaven, prepared as a Bride adorned for her husband.

(Revelation 21:2)

Revelation 21:11 describes the materials in the New Jerusalem.

Having the glory of God and her light was like unto a stone most precious even like a jasper stone, clear as crystal.

Thank God that we are the New Jerusalem in the Earth. Revelation 21:18-21 further elaborates on what heaven will look like.

And the building of the wall of it was of jasper: and the city was pure gold, like unto clear glass. And the foundations of the wall of the city were garnished with all manner of precious stones. The first foundation was jasper; the second, sapphire; the third, a chalcedony; the fourth, an emerald; The fifth, sardonyx; the sixth, sardius; the seventh, chrysolite; the eighth, beryl; the ninth, a topaz; the tenth, a chrysoprasus; the eleventh, a jacinth; the twelfth, an amethyst. And the twelve gates were twelve pearls; every several gate was of one pearl: and the street of the city was pure gold, as it were transparent glass.

God clearly is not against precious jewels and gold since

He used it to adorn His Kingdom!

While God has prepared for us a place we cannot even imagine called "heaven," He has also instituted a system of blessing us here on earth. See Deuteronomy 28:1-14...these verses explain in great detail God's system for blessing obedience.

When you obey God, these verses make it clear that He wants to reward, bless, and prosper you. But the world has corrupted the concept of money and prosperity by kicking God out of their lives and instead making money their god. But clearly, Scripture reveals over and over that...

Wealth, abundance, favor, grace and money is God's idea for you!

I know you will be glad to know that in the New Heaven and New Earth to come there will be no need for a money economy as we know it. Hallelujah! I just want to look upon His face.

However, since we are confronted with two economies each day of our lives, one being the world's system of finance and the other being the Heavenly Economy, we must understand that they operate from different principles. Which economy are you operating in?

The World's Economy

The world operates their finances in the following manner:

1. Illegal, such as cheating on income tax returns.
2. Unethical, such as conflicts of interest.
3. Immoral, such as prostitution and gambling.
4. Cheating, lying and stealing.
5. Hurting people.
6. Climbing over people to get ahead.
7. Committing crimes such as robbery and office theft.

8. Many manipulate others to get money.
9. Take and never give.
10. Money controls these people.
11. A welfare system that keeps people dependent, and with their hands out.
12. Money is their god.

The Heavenly Economy

Now, let us look at God's Heavenly Economy and how it operates:

1. Anointings and grace.
2. Abilities.
3. Diversities of gifts.
4. Sowing and reaping.
5. Giving and receiving.
6. Investing and returning.
7. Seed time/harvest time.
8. Tithes and offerings.
9. Renewed mind and thoughts.

These are God's concepts and laws on finance. As you practice them, they will help you generate income streams, revenue and money. Our heavenly Father's campaign is to bring many sons unto glory. Money will help meet the needs of the people who you can help to bring into the Kingdom. **God wants us to recognize that whatever money we have is due to His goodness and mercy.**

The silver and gold is mine saith the Lord of host.
(Haggai 2:8)

The silver and gold belong to God. So, it is important that we recognize that a) God is our source, b) and all that is in the earth is for our pleasure and purposes. We don't need all of this silver and gold after physical death, we need it now.

If gold and silver means nothing to God, then why is it

mentioned in Haggai 2:8?

I am convinced that the major purpose of money and abundance is to help establish the covenant of God in the earth by bringing many sons unto glory. However, in the process, by you taking care of God's work in the earth with money, you benefit and are able to use some of the money, favor and materials for yourself.

The 100% Tithe

A tithe means a tenth, however, from a spiritual sense our lives should become a tithe and offering unto the Lord Jesus, the High Priest. He can possess 100% of me—not just 10% of my life—in heaven and in the earth. Jesus, the High Priest, can have 100% of my entire life (which puts me also in the Melchisedec Priesthood and lineage).

Releasing the anointing is a special grace from God to assist you in the earth so that you will be able to bless others through your grace giving. Whether you are giving out wisdom, abundance or money you will be able to give to others in an unprecedented way because of great grace has been bestowed on your life through the anointing.

Releasing the Money Anointing will take you beyond tithes and offerings into another level of uncommon giving or "grace giving" as described by Michael L. Webb and Mitchell T. Webb in their book entitled *Beyond Tithes and Offerings*. However, I don't agree with these authors who espouse that paying tithes or returning the tithe is no longer a practice that God supports today. Although, I do support their concept on "grace giving" and especially helping the poor.

We should honor God in everything we do even returning the tithe and offerings or giving uncommon financial seeds. However, the ultimate purpose of financial giving should be to bless people in the earth.

By this we come to know (progressively to recognize, to

perceive, to understand) *the [essential] love: that He laid down His [own] life for us; and we ought to lay [our] lives down for [those who are our] brothers [in Him]. But if anyone has this world's goods* (resources for sustaining life) *and sees his brother and fellow believer in need, yet closes his heart of compassion against him, how can the love of God live and remain in him?*

(1 John 3:16-17 Amplified Version))

Someone said, "We are no closer to God than we are to our brothers and sisters in the earth. All the wealth, materials, wisdom, knowledge and money we receive from the release of the anointing of grace should be given away to others as a demonstration of our love for God and our neighbors. (Mark 12:30-31, Amplified Version)

"And you shall love the Lord your God out of and with your whole heart and out of and with all your soul (your life) *and out of and with all your mind* (with your faculty of thought and your moral understanding) *and out of and with all your strength."* This is the first and principal commandment. (Deuteronomy 6:4-5)

The second is like it and is this, *"You shall love your neighbor as yourself. There is no commandment greater than these."* (Leviticus 19:18)

"Before Abraham Was, I Am"

Jesus was a type and shadow of Melchizedek, King of Salem (meaning peace.) Jesus Christ in Isaiah 9:6 is referred to as the prince of peace. "To us a Child is born, to us a Son is given; and the government shall be upon His shoulder, and His name shall be called Wonderful Counselor, Mighty God, Everlasting Father, Prince of Peace."

I often hear people say that they only return the tithes to a live man, like Abraham paid tithes to King Melchizedek in Genesis 14:18-20 and not through a local fellowship.

*And Melchizedek king of Salem brought forth bread
and wine: and he was the priest of the most high God.
And he blessed him, and said, Blessed be Abram of
the most high God, possessor of heaven and earth:
And blessed be the most high God, which hath
delivered thine enemies into thy hand. And he gave
him tithes of all.*

There are those who say you cannot honor a dead man or
invisible man like Jesus by honoring Him with tithes today.
If that is the case, then we cannot give worship to an
invisible God or praise to an invisible Jesus, or pray to an
invisible God. Everything we do should be to honor Christ
and even in the giving away our money to bless others. They
further say that Abraham should be our example today as it
relates to paying tithes to Melchizedek or a live man in the
earth. Jesus' statement can clear up this over emphasis on
Abraham and even Melchizedek in John 8:56, 58:

*Your father Abraham rejoiced to see my day: and he
saw it, and was glad.*

*Jesus said unto them, Verily, verily, I say unto you,
before Abraham was, I am.*

George Barna, in his book, *How to Increase Giving in
Your Church* (published by Regal Books, 1997), states the
following: "Just one-third of all born again Christians who
attend a church (35 percent) and one-fifth of non Christians
who attend a Christian church (22 percent), believe that the
Bible teaches us to tithe." Two out of three adults believe
the Bible offers suggestions about giving, but that it leaves
the final choice totally up to us. He further states that
whichever side of the controversy you choose to endorse, the
common ground is this: "God expects us to be generous
givers and to provide a generous share of our first-fruits for
His works."

Returning the tithe and giving offering is a minimum
start, a standard, a principle and a guideline for future

"grace giving" to help so many other people through corporate giving and/or individual giving. Tithing opens the window to give offerings to also bless others. For those who return the tithe to a visible man, apostle or spiritual father should not condemn those who don't. There are those who choose to honor an invisible Christ by returning their tithe to a local fellowship or local church. These people should not be told they are not going to be blessed because they are in the wrong lineage. Because they are not in your personal lineage, it doesn't mean they are cursed. Every tither is automatically in the lineage of Christ as a result of their New Birth. If you are a set man, apostle or spiritual father, just be honest and tell your sons and daughters that you need money and/or financial support instead of using the Abrahamic and Melchizedek principle to hide behind and create guilt and shame in your sons and daughters who don't return the tithe to you. Finally, whether you return the tithe to a spiritual father or a set man or local church make certain that you honor the Lord first in your heart in all that you do with the tithe. I strongly support the returning of the tithe and the offerings.

I really don't have any problems returning honor to a set man, a spiritual father, giving honor to that person as a result of receiving spiritual impartation from them. I understand the tithing system really was for the Levite priesthood.

Appreciate God's Gifts

God owes us nothing other than what He has promised us in His Word. That is why it is vital that we recognize and walk in a deep appreciation of what God has done in our lives.

Appreciate the opportunity your finances give you to take part in ministry and apostleship, according to Acts 1:25. Appreciate what an honor and privilege it is to not only experience apostleship, but to be able to support other ministries as you are able.

*By whom we have received grace and apostleship, for
obedience to the faith among all nations, for His name.*
(Romans 1:5)

Appreciate what God is doing in your life, and if you have
ungodly attitudes towards money, realize that your heart for
money should be to support your family, to help others, and
to establish the covenant of God.

As you receive more money, keep allowing the Holy Spirit
to adjust and protect your motives. They must be right as
God flows His blessings into your life.

You see, money can be good or bad. There are bad people
with money and God's people with money. The Word
declares it is the "love of money" that is "the root of all evil."
With the right motive, you can thank God for bringing
money into your life...without loving it.

God Knows Money is Important

Money is important to God according to Malachi 3:8-10:

*Will a man rob God? Yet ye have robbed me. But ye
say, Wherein have we robbed thee? In tithes and
offerings. Ye are cursed with a curse: for ye have
robbed me, even this whole nation. Bring ye all the
tithes into the storehouse.*

Money is important because it allows us to be a blessing to
others, support our families, promote the proclamation of the
Kingdom of God, and support the apostolic work.

God desires that we be "money masters", and not allow
our money to master us! He knows money is important
because without money we will be limited in achieving the
purposes of God in the earth. The kingdom of heaven is
compared to merchant men. Merchant men are money men.

If you do not believe money is important, try living
without money for 30 days!

Money does bring us supply and power and we must never allow money to rule our lives.

Receive money without loving it.

Recognize the power of money without worshipping it.

You create a Godly, wealthy place when you seek His face. Put God first!

God's heavenly economy is established to overturn the world's economy of wealth into our hands as the sons and daughters of God.

Don't Curse the Seed!

Don't curse the seed that you plan to sow. Don't curse money!

If a corn farmer got up every morning and cursed his corn seed by saying, "I really don't care about corn," then he should not expect much of a harvest. Or, if a watermelon farmer cursed his watermelon seeds by saying, "I'm really sick and tired of harvesting watermelon," then this farmer has nothing to complain about if all the watermelons in his field are destroyed that year.

Likewise, do not curse the financial seed that you plan to sow. If you talk against or bash the purpose of the financial seed you plant, you will not receive a harvest for yourself or the people you are trying to help.

Negative cursing hinders your prosperity.

If you talk negatively about sowing your money or finances to help bring the Gospel of the Kingdom to Europe, then do not except a harvest of souls, or sons and daughters of God, in Europe. Do not sow your seed grudgingly.

God loveth a cheerful giver!

(2 Corinthians 9:7)

Dishonesty and
False Humility about Money

Be honest about your views on money; you cannot have it both ways. On one hand, many say, "money is not important to me." But you need it. Others say, "Money has no value for me." But yet they cannot live without it.

Do you see the contradiction?

Stop sending a double message to people. If money is not important to you, and you do not need to ever receive anymore money, or work anymore, or buy food any more, then maybe you can make these declarations. However, I don't know how you could accomplish this since we all need to at least buy food.

Christians need to start admitting that money is important, and then start handling the money we receive responsibly. When you are double-minded about money, it shows that you are not being really honest, and are trying to live with a false humility about money.

Money really means a whole lot to you, so we need to be honest about it. If you lie about money, you will lie about anything!

Money can be good or bad, but you may have a bad attitude toward money. Money takes on the personality of a bad or good person. Money is not attracted to double-minded people who have these strange views on money. Money runs from you because you do not think it is important. People do not sow into your life because of this spirit of error. Money is not attracted to you because you are not a money master; instead, you are a money basher. Money is afraid of you. It runs from you because you undermine your own money and wealth. People do not sow into your life on a regular basis because people do not want to offend you. Since money runs from you, you will always lack, have wants, and fall behind in money because you are a money basher.

Stop being dishonest about money. Tell the truth. Say out loud, "Money is important to me." Bring an end to your false humility about money which will ultimately lead to illegal, unethical, or immoral behavior which leads to begging.

Those who are dishonest about money will try to make you feel guilty about having money since they deny that your money has any value or premium. Those who are dishonest about the importance of money usually explain away the issue of money, and usually end up begging and borrowing money from their friends and relatives.

We cannot fight the apostolic warfare in Iraq without money. Try to fight a military war without money. You won't have any soldiers to fight for you. President Bush has requested over $80 billion dollars for the Iraq war and rebuilding program. I support President Bush.

Money answereth all things.

(Ecclesiastes 10:19)

There are some things you do not have now because you do not have money. You cannot help send out a missionary team to South Africa because you do not have the money. You cannot get medical aid to all the dying people in Africa because you do not have any money. If you had money, it could help someone else.

Expecting a Return on Your Seed

Sowing is biblical, and will always produce a harvest. You should not feel guilty or condemned about having money as a result of faithful sowing. Expect a return for you, and for the person you are helping as a result of giving away or sowing your money as a seed. Pay a hospital bill, help someone through college, help someone come to Christ...all and more can be the increase and return on your financial sowing.

The return may not always be money. But, bringing many sons unto glory and getting people saved is an even greater return. You can, from time-to-time, sow a financial seed and expect a return of materials, favor, or wisdom for you or others.

Every Seed Begets After its Own Kind

If you plant watermelon seeds, you will get a watermelon harvest. If you plant corn seeds, you will get corn. Potato seeds produce potatoes. Money seed produces a harvest of money and materials.

Conversely, if you plant grace to others, you will receive grace in return. Plant love and others will love you. Plant hope and you will never be without it.

Sow your money with a purpose in mind. Determine in your heart to sow money to help others.

The Bottom Line

You have the power to release your money in the earth through your anointing. Releasing the money anointing will change or transform your life, and bring you into receiving money on a regular basis without sweating or work. You can create your own money through the anointing on your life.

You are the wealth of God, which is the key to money being magnetized or attracted to you. I believe this book will help the presidents of corporations who are in financial stress to turn their businesses around. To help in that area, I will offer company group rates to all who want to buy this book in volume.

The principles contained in this book will help pastors to generate revenue for ministry, and increase more income among the congregation. Every pastor should have their congregation read this book. They will see greater revenue, increases in tithing, offerings, and new businesses will spring up in their congregations.

Let's face a simple fact: You have greater joy when you have money to help others and yourself.

My prayer is that your anointing flows so powerfully that you will enter into a place where you will never have to worry again about money coming into your life.

Expecting Miracles from God's Word

We, as Christians, are expecting.

"What are we expecting?" you ask.

We are expecting wealth, abundance, prosperity, and success for YOU in the Kingdom of God...right now, this year!

Expectancy involves a pregnancy.

God is spiritually impregnating His people with "sperma," the New Testament Greek word for "seed." The Word of God is the seed or sperma that must get inside of you (Mark 4:14, James 1:21, Mark4:26-32). God's Word is called the seed of reproduction in Luke 8:11. God's Word reproduces life, wealth, abundance, prosperity, and success (Luke 8:5, Mark 4:27).

You already are pregnant with the seed of God's Word. You are already spiritually pregnant with the sperma of God because the Word of God makes you pregnant by the spirit of God. The Word of God will make you pregnant with wealth, abundance, prosperity, and success. God has already impregnated you with spiritual and financial wealth, and divine and material wealth because the very seed of these things are in the Word, and His Word is in you to do His work.

When a woman is pregnant, she is expecting to give birth and release that baby into the earth as a living, breathing person. So, either you are pregnant or not; either you are spiritually pregnant or you are not.

If we are spiritually pregnant, then we must act on that fact and expect the birth and release of our spiritual baby, be it financial, material, a healing, deliverance, or whatever it is. **It is possible to abort the spiritual pregnancy by embracing doubt and unbelief.**

With the Word of God deeply rooted, grounded, and implanted in your heart, you can expect the birth of spiritual babies. "Expecting" really means you anticipate your release, thinking about the manifestation.

You believe it will happen!

You look forward to it, wait eagerly and watch for it, and you tell everyone else about it. In any state of expectancy you have to be ready to receive and be prepared for the birth of what you need from God.

Remember the principle: first physical, then spiritual.

Get ready to receive the baby of wealth, the baby of prosperity, the baby of success, the baby of abundance.

We are not wanting to get pregnant, we already are pregnant by the Word of God! And, the Word of God prepares us for the "delivery" by its constant and consistent entrance into our spirits (Romans 10:17).

You do not need to want anything (Psalms 23:1)! You are **already implanted** with God's Word which will deliver the spiritual baby. Wanting means that you do not have it. You would love to have it, but wanting implies you are deprived of something. Wanting means that you are incomplete, insufficient, that you are lacking and short of what you desire.

You can desire spiritual blessings and never experience them. You can need more income and never have it. You can desire wealth and never experience it. You can seek after abundance but never enjoy it. You can want prosperity and never live in it. Desire success and never obtain it.

You can desire a spiritual pregnancy from the sperma of God, and never get pregnant.

Receive God's Word; absorb His seed into your heart. As you do, He will implant His Word in you to grow; the manifestation will come. Wanting will never bring the physical manifestations of the baby. We are not wanting, we are expecting as a natural result of our spiritual pregnancy the release and birth of the physical manifestations of wealth, abundance, prosperity, and success.

And, because God's Word always produces, our expectations will be manifested in this physical earth.

The Wealth of King Jesus

According to the Word of God, Jesus walked in the covenant of God, living a sinless life. Because He was in covenant with God, He would have experienced wealth. Everything He did was based on that covenant with God, so all the promises of the Old Testament were His. God's covenant with King Jesus was established here on earth by God's Word (Deuteronomy 8:18).

Jesus was and is spiritually wealthy!
Jesus was and is financially wealthy!
Jesus was and is physically wealthy!
Jesus was and is materially wealthy!

We know that Jesus was and is spiritually wealthy because the Word says that the fullness of the Godhead indwells Him (Colossians 2:9), that all fullness dwells in Him (Colossians 1:19), that all things are under His feet (1 Corinthians 15:27; Ephesians 1:22), that He holds the keys of the Kingdom (Revelation 1:18), and that He is the first and the last, the Alpha and Omega (Revelation 1:8, 21:6, 22:13). In the first part of John 14, we see that Jesus and His Father, our Father, is preparing mansions for us in the new Kingdom to be set up.

The Father's house is really the Church, and in the Church there are indeed many mansions. God, our Father, has set up four distinct mansions here on this earth through His Kingdom: spiritual mansions, financial mansions, divine health mansions and material mansions. While Jesus was here on earth, He lived in His Father's spiritual house. Now He has returned to His heavenly house so He can enjoy the Father's house here on earth, the Church (John 14).

There will always be those who want to glory in the presumption that King Jesus was poor on this earth. There are some Scriptures that would seem to imply that concept. It is true that there was a point in time when He had nothing. But ultimately, even the clothes He wore became objects of envy to the Roman soldiers who were willing to contest who should receive them (John 19:23-24).

Jesus always had whatever He needed to accomplish what He intended to do. He even had a treasurer for his ministry, and enough money in that treasury to tempt Judas to steal from it (John 13:29). Jesus had a support structure large enough to support Him and His disciples, and even had money left over to give to the poor (Luke 8:1, Acts 20:35). At the scene of the feeding of the five thousand, He told the disciples to give the people what they needed. It was the disciples who protested that they only had a few fish and a few loaves of bread (Matthew 14:15-20 and Luke 9:13).

Jesus had a house to live in, and He had visitors in that home, at least in the beginning of His ministry before He went on the road (Matthew 13:1, 9:28, 13:36, John 1:35-39).

His ministry was supported by His own "city church" or local group of people (Luke 8:3, Mark 15:40-41). Even His disciples were impressed with Him when He told them to follow Him. Levi saw Him and got right up from the table at his job and followed Him (Luke 5:27-28).

Jesus Had Material Wealth

Some try to explain away these Scriptures and say that King Jesus was poor and had nothing, but this is just not true to Scripture.

The enemy wants you to stay poor and not have the things God has already provided for you. There are people that want to keep you spiritually poor, financially poor, physically poor, and materially poor. Jesus was not spiritually poor, He is the fullness of God. Jesus was not financially poor, He had a support structure. Jesus was not physically poor, He walked in divine health. Jesus was not materially poor, He had what He needed.

There are some Scriptures people will use to support the idea that we should be poor, stay broke, and remain in poverty. They maintain poverty keeps you closer to God and brings glory to Him. The misinterpretation of these Scriptures is in some people's plan to keep you right where you are in your wrong thinking. Let us look at several questions frequently asked, and respond to them in the light of the entire Word of God and their own context.

Question # 1:

"If Jesus was not poverty stricken, why didn't He have a place to sleep or lay down His head?" (See Luke 9:51-58)

When you consider the Scriptures already presented in this book on the financial integrity of King Jesus, and when you look at the context of this particular Scripture, you can see that He was unwelcome in that village and had nowhere to stay in that town. No one offered Him a place to stay. No one wanted His headship or governments in their lives.

Question # 2:

"Peter and John had no silver and gold. Doesn't this mean that Christians should be financially poor? (See Acts 3:1-9)

First of all, when you understand the customs of the time, you know that this statement was not true. Peter and John had to have money to get into the temple. They were on Jesus' staff (Luke 10:7), and on their way to the temple to pray. Whenever you went to the temple in those days, you would go with an offering which was given into the treasury at the door. Even the poor came with some kind of money offering to the temple in Jerusalem (Mark 12:41-44). The reason they said they had no "silver and gold" is because they brought only enough money for their offering that day.

Question # 3:

"Jesus was poor. Shouldn't we, as Christians, be poor?" (See 2 Corinthians 8:9)

First, look at this Scripture in its own context, then compare it with other Scriptures such as John 18:36, Daniel 4:17, Colossians 2, Philippians 2, Romans 5, Hebrews 6-9, and numerous portions of the book of Revelation. Jesus became poor to this world's system, and according to this world's system, He was poor. He did not make this world His source. God, the Father, was His source. King Jesus was rich! All that He needed was provided when He needed it. We now become rich because we make God, the Father, our source. And we are joint heirs with King Jesus to receive all that God has for us (Romans 8:17, Galatians 3:29, 4:1,7, 30, Ephesians 3:6, Titus 3:7, Hebrews 1:14, James 2:5). We are now heirs of that new covenant, ratified by the death and resurrection of the Lord Jesus Christ, our King. By any system standard, King Jesus has returned to heaven and He is not poor anymore; He is ready and willing to supply our needs, not according to our need or want or desire, but according to His riches (Philippians 4:19, Deuteronomy 8:10).

Question # 4:

"I thought Jesus instructed us to sell all that we have and give to the poor?" (See Matthew 19:21)

We must realize that the situation in this Scripture was real, and the person Jesus was talking to was real. It was not just a story. Jesus was not poor, so why would He have wanted this person to be poor? Jesus wanted this man to focus in on the problem. The man wanted to follow Jesus, but he wanted to do it on his own terms. He did not want to give up his money or possessions. This man's "things" possessed him, and Jesus pinpointed that issue. His things had him in so much bondage that he could not let go enough to obey Christ and follow Him by helping the poor. If this man would have done what Jesus had asked him to do, he would have been able to trust God completely and rely on the Father as his total source, trusting Him for his financial sustenance.

If God can get your money, He has you. Your money is part of you. You have your time, effort, and energy into the money that you make. This man said he loved God, and Jesus simply challenged him to give up his wealth and demonstrate his commitment.

Financial wealth is based on three key principles:

1. Give yourself to God.
2. Give your money to God by helping others.
3. Steward what God has given to you.

Matthew 6:21 states that where your treasure is, there will your heart be. Your heart determines the treasure!

CHAPTER ELEVEN

Three Secrets of Wealth and Abundance

Remember that wealth and abundance are to help establish God's covenant in this earthly realm.

> *But thou shall remember the Lord thy God, for it is he that gives thee power to get wealth, that he may establish his covenant which he swore unto thy fathers, as it is this day.*
>
> (Deuteronomy 8:18)

Wealth is ordained by God, the Father! The very nature of one of His names represents the provision of wealth: Jehovah Jireh, the Lord that provides. The Lord's provisions for His children will be evident and seen in plenty, riches, and prosperity.

Abundance or surplus is ordained by God, the Father. One of His names means the God who is more than enough. The Almighty God, El-Shaddai, was wealth and abundance to Abraham, Isaac, and Jacob. Abundance is having more than enough spiritually, financially, physically and materially. The New Testament reaffirms this concept in Ephesians 3:20-21.

Prosperity is ordained by God. Prosperity includes wealth, abundance, and good success (Joshua 1:9). The Word of God promises good success when the Word is implanted in the heart by meditation. Psalm 1:3 says:

> *And he shall be like a tree planted by the rivers of water, that bringeth forth is fruit in his season; his*

leaf also shall not wither; and whatsoever he doeth shall prosper.

Do you see it? This passage means that whatever a righteous man does, he will prosper.

This means that whatever you do, you should realize success and prosperity. Your job, marriage, children, health, and even the community you live in should be in prosperity. You should be a blessing, an influence in your community and church...wherever God chooses to put you.

God has already granted you Kingdom wealth and abundance through King Jesus. His work for you on the cross and His resurrection bought you your Kingdom rights. By His Word, you are born rich in and by the spirit of God. It is by His grace and nothing you have done.

Then he answered and spoke unto me saying, not by might, not by power, but by my spirit, saith the Lord.
(Zechariah 4:6)

Also see Ephesians 2 and Romans 8.

Now is your time to receive what God has already provided for you. Through the Word of God, and by His spirit, you are wealthy, full of abundance and very prosperous. These have been decreed by the King Himself, Jesus.

Secret Number One:
Use Your God-Given Imagination

The first secret to wealth and abundance is to begin to use the imagination God has given you to create your wealth and abundance. Through your imagination you have the seeds to begin possessing your wealth and abundance. God, Himself, imagined man before He created him (see Genesis 1:26-27, 5:3, 9:6).

Second Corinthians 10:5 instructs us to cast down imaginations and things that exalt themselves against the knowledge of God. We must cast down those negative and bondage thoughts of poverty, sickness, lack, evil, and death. We must begin to realize who we are in Jesus.

Accept that fact and receive it!

We must all become positive image—makers by and in the Word of God. Begin to see yourself as having all that God has for you. Use your imagination to visualize and picture yourself as the person God has ordained and declared you to be (2 Corinthians 4:18).

You must declare and decree with your mouth what God has already declared and decreed you to be (Job 22: 28).

In Romans 4:17, Abraham acted as God and declared those things which are not as though they were. His very name was a declaration of faith as he and others said it, since he was "the father of many nations."

Don't allow problems or circumstances to dictate your Kingdom destiny. Don't allow your checking account's low balance to define who you are. Don't let the bills piling up derail you from your spiritual success. Your spiritual success will dictate the physical success.

Don't allow negative Christians or family members to influence your thinking, and eventually, your future. Use the spiritual success God has put in you through His Word and by His Spirit to conquer poverty, sickness, and the circumstances of life that want to crush you.

Every name that is named will one day be under the feet of King Jesus...that means under your feet too (Psalm 8:6, Romans 8:37, Galatians 6:13). So, put all things that are not of God under your feet (1 Corinthians 15:25,27, Ephesians 1:22). You must take the images that God gives you and obtain your wealth and abundance in the spirit realm. Then, move it into the physical realm for the physical manifestation.

God, the Father, has given you the ability to make and create in your heart and mind.

For as he thinketh in his heart, so is he:

(Proverbs 23:7)

Think spiritual wealth. Think financial wealth and abundance. Think material and physical wealth.

Jesus said that what a person thinks within himself, that is what he is. Out of the heart comes the things that are inside a person (Matthew 12:35-37). Think about who you are and who God has made you to be. Regardless of how hard the situations of life may appear to be, remember that they are temporal and given to change (2 Corinthians 4:18).

Hold fast to the prosperity image that God has given you. Be a believer (1 Corinthians 15:57-58, Ephesians 6:13). All things are spiritual. Healing—money—success—material gain are spiritual.

If you need healing, you must see yourself healed. If you need material gain, you must first see yourself with material gain. If you need money, you must first see yourself with money. If you need a new job, see it before you actually have it.

This principle of seeing yourself as God sees you and wants you to be, declared and decreed by His word to be so, applies to all of life. It applies to your business prospering, your marriage happy and full of joy, your children content and full of wisdom, your finances set in order and abundant, your personal inner-peace, your feelings about yourself as accurate and positive.

Now, reverse these actions to see where you have missed the principle, and have put into motion a negative force against the very things you desire in your life. If you are sick, you may have seen yourself as sick and "unhealable." If your business is failing, you may have seen and declared it so. If you do not have enough money, you may have declared it to be so. If you do not feel good about yourself naturally, then you do not feel good about yourself spiritually. If you are in doubt and unbelief, then those thoughts transfer to the things of God.

What you are in the spirit realm will manifest itself in the physical realm. If you entertain worry, uncertainty, failure, insecurity, and stress, it will reflect in both realms for you.

Secret Number Two:
Expect God to Honor His Word

The second secret to wealth and abundance is to operate in the expectation that God will honor His Word as a daily process. Expect God to send into your life the images you have developed. Picture your financial miracles daily and thank God for them. Visualize your financial miracles daily and thank God for them. Thank God daily for your spiritual manifestations, your financial manifestations, your physical manifestations, and your material manifestations. Your *faith imagination* in the spiritual realm will take your abilities, your power, your abundance, your strength, and the things God has for you, and will produce them in the physical realm (Hebrews 2:4, Acts 19:11, 1 Corinthians 12:10).

Manifestations occur in the church to benefit heirs of God–true Christians (1 Corinthians 12:28, Galatians 3:5, Hebrews 2:4).

Secret Number Three:
Give to Produce Prosperity

The third secret to wealth and abundance is perhaps the hardest to understand. We must demonstrate and show the power of God in out-giving. We do not give to get, but we give because it is God's command and His principle of life.

Hording does not help you keep your riches. Giving is the way to prosperity.

The tithe (Malachi 3:10) is God's principle, and is also established in the New Testament in the latter half of the book of Hebrews. Ten percent of your gross income is the Lord's.

Then come offerings (Luke 6:38). They establish the measure that God is able to give back to you. If you sow small, then you will reap small. As you give into God's Kingdom, He will replenish and give back to you.

Micro giving equals micro receiving.

You cannot talk about giving without talking about receiving. They are one in the same with God, it's a law. He is a giving God and wants you to be ready to receive. Your financial seed is one way to represent your faith toward God. You are planting your faith when you give into your local church or ministry (Galatians 6:7-9). You are also planting that seed to grow, and not to just lay there in the ground and rot. Your money seed will produce because God has set in order the laws of giving and receiving, sowing and reaping (Genesis 8:22, Ecclesiastes 3:1).

The kind of seed you plant will be the kind of harvest you will receive.

Plant money to get money. Plant clothes to get clothing. Plant healing to receive healing. The way you plant and the measure you meet out will be the measure God uses to measure back to you (Luke 6:38b).

Imagine what God has given you and see it in your spirit. Expect daily miracles from God. As He provides, thank Him. And, demonstrate your faith by giving into God's Kingdom.

CHAPTER TWELVE

Receive the Anointing and Be Transformed!

Do you believe that your day, your hour, your time, your season has come? Not tomorrow, not next week, but right now?

The just shall live by faith...right now!

Praying and hoping are not faith. Faith is *acting* on God's Word. Faith is taking a risk and trusting God at His Word. Faith is not praying and fasting, then waiting for God to do something.

Faith is acting and trusting God now.

Stop waiting on God...He is waiting on you to realize it is your time to release the money anointing and experience the freedom He desires for you.

That is why it is vital to listen to how the Apostle Paul shares how to release the money anointing.

> *I beseech you therefore, brethren, by the mercies of God, that ye present your bodies a living sacrifice, holy, acceptable unto God, which is your reasonable service. And be not conformed to this world: but be ye transformed by the renewing of your mind, that ye may prove what is that good, and acceptable, and perfect, will of God.*
>
> (Romans 12:1-2)

Present Your Body to God

To receive a release from God, the first thing you must do is to *present your body* to the Lord as a living sacrifice, as a holy body. God will reject a fornicating body, an adulterous body, a pornographic body, a rebellious body, or even an independent body. He is seeking a body that is *holy, acceptable unto God, which is your reasonable* (normal) *service.*

We must keep our bodies sanctified and holy before the Lord, not conformed to this age, to the lifestyles of this world. We must conform our lives to knowing that the God is our source.

Be Ye Transformed

The word "transform" comes from the Greek word *"metamorpho"* which means " to change." Your money anointing is directly dependent upon your transformation. Your ability to change your negative thoughts to God thoughts.

As you know (if you've been a good student), when we talk about releasing your anointing, we are talking about releasing it in all four areas we have covered in this book: Shemen, Christos, Pneuma, and Rhema.

To release any of these anointings into your life, especially the money anointing, you must be transformed by the constant renewing and transformation of your thought life. This world is full of mind pollution and trash for the soul. It is full of filth and doubt. Depictions on television undermine parents, undermine the Church, undermine the Kingdom of God. The world tries to pollute your mind through pornographic Web sites. (Of course, the Web can also be used for God.)

Renew your mind, moment by moment. Notice I did not write, "day-by-day." You cannot renew your mind *only* in the morning and in the evening...you must *constantly* renew and renovate your mind, second-by-second, minute-by-minute, until you are changed and trans-figured.

If you want to change, you want to change *now*, not when you get to heaven.

As a Christian, you are already walking in heavenly places. As you continue to change and walk closer to God, the world needs to see you as a manifested son of God. As you manifest, you will release the spirit of adoption and the spirit of redemption. You will walk throughout this earth and everybody you touch will be changed in some way!

Start to ask the Holy Spirit how you can renew your mind and emotions. Your emotions are important. You cannot allow your emotions to run off with your mind. If your emotions and thoughts are not right, you will send the wrong message to the anointing. When you are acting freaky, the anointing cannot release that which you want.

Renew your thoughts. Study to show yourself approved. Read the Word of God on a daily basis. Let it expand your mind. Read literature and other books to learn and expand your thoughts in a variety of subjects so you can know what is going on in the world.   Understand global warfare, psychological warfare, and spiritual warfare. Expand your thoughts so you can receive the revelations of God.

It is also important to monitor and renew your feelings so they stay holy and sanctified. If your feelings are not godly, you will not be able to feel the anointing when it comes upon you. You will send the wrong message as the anointing of the Lord tries to break loose in you. You will not know how to read its code when your feelings are not right because of ungodly thoughts, a mood swing, a sugar swing or depression.

Renew your thought life and bring it into subjection. Bring your thoughts into captivity!

Renew. Renew. Renew!

Renew the images you have in your mind. If your images are not right, if your thoughts are not right, if your feelings are not right, if your intellect is not right, if your emotions are not right, you will send the wrong message to the anointing.

The anointing can only operate by faith. When your images, thoughts, feelings, intellect, and emotions are not right, you send the wrong message, and the anointing says, "I can't compute. I don't know what they are saying. Are they saying that their body needs to be healed? Are they saying they need money? Are they saying they need love? I don't know what they are saying."

Renew and saturate your being with the Word of God so the anointing can touch and communicate to you. That will spark the process of renewing and renovating your mind, your brain, your intellect, your emotions, thoughts, and feelings, purging you of those things you should not have or experience.

The releasing of the anointing is based upon the renewing of the mind and the releasing of new thoughts!

Renew your mind with new wine and new wine skins. Start to drink what God is saying now as He updates His people. God is now dealing with the royal priesthood, the righteousness of God. We are the manifest sons of God, and He is now updating us on how to transform the earth.

He is renewing our minds with the new oil, the new revelation, the deep things of God.

Deeper, Deeper, Deeper!

Call on God and ask Him to come and go deeper into you. Let your feelings, and your thoughts call out, "God, come and go deeper into me."

He wants to come, but you need to prepare yourself to receive Him by renewing your thoughts, your images and your intellect so He can get down in there and pour out the anointing oil.

Releasing the money anointing is transformation, but you must *do something in faith* to activate that transformation and change. You are *only* required to do *one thing* to bring about the transformation...renew your mind or thoughts.

If you will renew your mind, and go deeper into Him, the shemen, the christos, the pneuma, and the rhema will flow into your life.

The releasing of the anointing is the transformation!

Another way to receive the anointing and contain it is to renew your mind (which consists of will, emotions, intellect, thoughts, soul). The releasing of the anointing is the change you have been expecting so you can begin to receive your money, wealth and abundance.

The Anointing is the Change

The anointing helps change the way you think.

The anointing helps change your emotions.

The anointing is not going to occupy a bad mind that is shaky and unstable. You may have God, you may have Jesus on the inside listening to what your spirit is saying, but your mind or thoughts void of the anointing of God.

If you know Jesus Christ as your personal Savior, your spirit is saved. You have been regenerated by the Holy Spirit. However, you can be saved and still be freaky, psychotic, or mentally ill. Why? Because your spirit is saved, not your soul. The anointing is not going to occupy a bad mind or thoughts.

If your mind is drug-infested, or is a poverty stricken mind, or a lying mind, then you are not going to receive a money anointing. The releasing of the money anointing is the transformation within itself. So, the clear answer to

"How do I receive the anointing?" is simply "Renew your mind." Renew your thoughts.

You cannot continue to think the way you have always thought. "If you keep on doing what you have always done, you will keep getting what you always have got."

That statement answers many questions.

"Charles Winburn, why do I end up with all these crazy men in my life?"

If you keep on doing what you have always done, you will keep getting what you always have got. You attract these people through your thoughts. The law of draw.

"Why am I still overweight?"

If you keep on doing what you have always done, you will keep getting what you always have got.

"Why do I have these painful migraines all the time?"

If you keep on doing what you have always done, you will keep getting what you always have got.

"Why am I so nervous all the time?"

If you keep on doing what you have always done, you will keep getting what you always have got. It happens through the law of draw. You draw to you what's in you. You attract to you what's in you.

You are sick all the time because you keep doing the same, wrong things all the time. You are broke all the time because you keep doing the same, wrong things all the time.

Releasing the money anointing is the change, the transformation within itself. Imagine...just by reading this book you are placing yourself in a position of transformation.

CHAPTER THIRTEEN

How to Use the Anointing
You Already Have

When I first started preaching this message in the local fellowship, the house was definitely shaken. Many poor people left because they did not want to become all that God had in store for them. Some said, "I will come back when Charles Winburn stops teaching on money, and moves on to another topic."

Money can be used for greedy, selfish reasons, but in the hands of a well-trained Christian, money is a powerful weapon, a practical tool for greatness and good.

Recently, a person in our fellowship blessed me with hundreds of dollars. I then planted some of that seed money into another person who was standing nearby. That money became a tool to bless someone else. That money answered someone else's prayers, enabling them to make a little investment.

Poverty is Misunderstood

I am not going to be a part of a poor church. If you are poor, you do not have to be poor any more. People are poor in spirit and broken. This does not mean poverty, it means to be broken in spirit. Yet Jesus was never poor, sick or broke.

If you want to be like Jesus, then you must begin to understand that poverty is a curse, not a blessing. God is not blessing His people with poverty, sickness and premature death.

To know the heart of God, we must read and honor Him through His Word.

> *But thou shalt remember the LORD thy God: for it is he that giveth thee power to get wealth, that he may establish his covenant which he sware unto thy fathers, as it is this day.*
>
> (Deuteronomy 8:18)

We are destined to be the wealth of God! If we are the wealth of God, then wealth plus wealth equals wealth. If we are the wealth of God, then we have the power to receive material wealth: money. We also have the favor of God to receive wisdom, influence, health, and prosperity.

If God is going to establish His covenant, it will be here on the earth! And to accomplish that purpose, He gives us the power to get wealth!

Friend, your wealth, your health, your prosperity, your influence, your favor, and your wisdom are coming!

You have been waiting on this moment, on this time, on this hour, on this second. It is your time to be healed, to receive wealth, to experience abundance in the presence of the Lord.

Use What You Already Have

Please understand: You are not trying to receive the anointing...you already have it! You cannot be anointed any higher than Shemen, the anointing of God Himself. You cannot be anointed any higher than the God of Abraham Himself anointing you.

You are already anointed with Shemen, with Christos, with Pneuma (the Holy Ghost), with Rhema (the Word of God).

You cannot fail in your finances, in your love life, in your family, in your community life. It is impossible for you to fail because of the anointing.

Now, unto Him that is able to keep you from falling and to present you in flawless before the presence of His glory with exceeding joy to the only wise God, our Savior; be glory, majesty, dominion and power. Now and forever and ever.

(1 Peter 4:11)

You may feel dead, but God is not. You may look like you are half off, but God is not off at all. As you use the anointing you already have, your life will break through all the hurdles.

When your father and mother conceived you, there were billions of tiny sperm cells, all trying to get to the egg. But only one could penetrate the egg. You are the result of that incredible process! There is something in your heritage that can push through life and circumstances against incredible odds. You can do all things through Christ that strengthens you.

Billions of other sperm cells failed, but you got through!

And, you can get through the hurdles of life you face today because you have the anointing.

Overcoming Hurdles

There are certain hurdles in life that will hinder your money from flowing. There is money that needs to get through, but something is holding that money back. You need to find out what you are doing wrong that is causing money not to come into your life on a regular basis. Sometimes listening to a negative pastor, a negative preacher, or even negative friends can hold up your money.

Remember, in Christ you are able to push through, to have revenue and money coming in because you understand that money is a good weapon, used for godly purposes, to help establish the covenant of God.

Of course, we have made a moral choice not to obtain money illegally through robbery or deception. We are not

231

going to get immoral or unethical money through prostitution, the selling of drugs, or by cheating on our income taxes.

We seek the money God has released to us through the anointing. We are going to get everything God has promised us in His Word, and we do not have to cheat to get it! We do not have to play bingo or win the lottery to get it. God did not promise us prosperity through gambling. But He promise that if we obey Him, we shall eat the fat of the land. He promised that He would give us the power to get wealth, to have favor, to have healing and strategic influence.

It is exciting when you have the anointing of God in your life!

Now, let me identify some of the hurdles that can stop money from flowing into your life today.

Hurdle One:

Not handling uncertainties properly will hinder your money flow.

Individuals seem to have a fear of the uncertain and unknown. But we are the anointed sons of God, so we are going to make it in this economy. If the whole earth tilts or shakes, if the world turns upside down, we are going to win! We are going to have everything that belongs to us because the earth is the Lord's, and the fullness thereof.

When you have fear of uncertainty, you are not living by faith. The just shall live by faith, not by fear of the uncertain. You must be willing to press through uncertainties, through the ambiguous, through the cloudy and unclear. You cannot always see your way through, so you must go forward by faith, not by what you see. When it is cloudy, you cannot see with your natural eye. You cannot even see your enemies in the natural until you put on your spiritual glasses. With spiritual glasses, you can see the enemies all around you, and you can see the angels of the Lord there to fight your battle.

With spiritual glasses, you will wait until everything is just right before you move out through the cloudy, through the storm and the rain.

You will walk through when it doesn't look like you are going to make it. You have been cultivating the land and there has not been any rain for six months. Keep working the land through the trials, the attacks, the tribulations and misunderstandings. Keep working the land until you hear the sound of the abundance of rain.

> *Charge them that are rich in this world, that they be not highminded, nor trust in uncertain riches, but in the living God, who giveth us richly all things to enjoy.*
>
> (1 Timothy 6:17)

Do not trust in uncertain riches. Do not worry about other peoples' money or wealth. Live by faith. Ignore uncertainty and press your way through. You fought to get to that egg that was in your mother, and today you keep fighting until you win, until you experience total victory.

Are you willing to fight through the fear of uncertainty?

Things are not certain all the time. If you could have your success up front, you would not need faith. If you could see everything you need at the time, you would not need faith.

You are not going to have any more fear of the uncertain. When the doctors give you a diagnosis of cancer, you are going to live by faith. When your boss gives you a pink slip and says, "Your job is over," you are going to live by faith. You will say, "They can turn this company upside down, but there is always a place for me on this earth because I am a manifested son of God. I don't care about the current uncertainty."

Your hope is built on nothing less than Jesus and His righteousness.

Your money and wealth are on the way. Your house and abundance are on the way. Say good-bye to the fear of uncertainty.

For if the trumpet give an uncertain sound, who shall prepare himself to the battle?

(1 Corinthians 14:8)

Do not live by uncertain sounds; move out in faith; listen to a certain sound from heaven. When the day of Pentecost was fully come, they were all in one accord and one place. Suddenly there came a sound from heaven. That is the sound you want to hear everyday...the sound that comes from heaven as a mighty, rushing wind.

Declare it now. "Lord, I want to hear Your sound, the sound of the abundance of rain."

You can overcome the fear of uncertainty without any medication. Meditate day and night on His Word. Say "good-bye" to the fear of uncertainty. It will not hinder your money anymore.

Hurdle Two:

Procrastination

Stop telling others that you are going into business one day, or that you are going to be wealthy one day. If you do not have it now, it never will be. If you are not working on it now, your faith is not now.

Faith is right now!

By faith, you have it now.

You are not trying to get it, you have it now. If you say, "I am going to loose weight one day," you are going to remain fat.

Declare what you can do now.

By faith, you are thin.

By faith, you are healed now, or you will never be healed.

You are wealthy now by faith, or you never will be. You are the wealth of God.

Procrastination will undermine the process. The Bible refers to procrastinators as "slow bellies." (Titus 1:11-12)

You are a liar if you do not obey the truth of God, because you are not who you say you are. Are you a slow belly? A slow belly in the Greek means "inactive"...you will not take an active stand, so you remain unemployed, lazy, useless, barren, and idle.

The Church is full of slow bellies.

If you are going to have money flowing, you cannot be slow about things. You must be ready to move in the place where God has called you to move. Slow bellies move too slowly in making key financial decisions. Delay after delay. You say, "I am going to start a business," and you never start one. You say, "I am going to be my own boss," yet you have stagnation after stagnation.

Make your soul behave! Begin to say, "I am not going to be stupid. I am the righteousness of God."

If you want money, you are going to have to press your way through. Slow bellies drag their feet. They do not have any short–or long–range goals. They are straddlers. They are not going to release money, wealth, or abundance because they straddle both ways.

You are either for God or the devil. You either choose life or death. You cannot straddle in the middle. Everybody must take a stand. You cannot be on both sides of the fence, flirting with the enemy on one side and working with God on the other. It doesn't work.

Procrastinators are the slow pokes in the Body of Christ. They miss out on money and power. They miss out on the wealth of God.

Say "good-bye" to procrastination. Some of you reading this book have been vowing to write your own book. You have been talking about doing that book for thirty years. You have waited so long that your message is outdated. Now, nobody will read a book that is thirty years old. Readers want to know what God is saying now—this year, this hour.

Bring an end to procrastination.

Hurdle Three:

Fear will stop your money flow even if you are a tither and give offerings.

I know many Christians who are faithful tithers, and give freely of their offerings, yet they still are without much money. Many are even broke. I know those who buy copious books and tapes, yet still have no money flowing into their lives. They attend great financial seminars, but there is still no money flow.

Something is wrong.

The problem is not with God, it is with you!

There's something in your life that is not part of God's plan, and it is holding up your anointing. Money is not flowing into your life because there are certain things you must constantly drive out of your life. You can return the tithe and still be broke. You can give offerings and still be broke because you are not giving it in faith. When you are living with the fear of uncertainty, and you have hesitation, when you come before God and are weak, you hinder God's flow.

You must come **boldly** before the Lord. You can't become intimidated. Even in the natural, when people come to me weakly, I ask myself, "Why are they bothering to approach me? They are coming to me with such a timid attitude. If they don't believe in their cause, then why should I?"

By coming to Him meekly and with insecurity, you actually provoke your Heavenly Father.

236

Stop blaming God for your mess in life.

God blessed you and has given you life. You better shake yourself and stop blaming God for what the devil has done and what you are doing with the devil. You are creating your own devil.

If you are able to lift both of your hands, you are doing wonderful in God. Stop blaming God for all this craziness. Clean up your life today so money can flow.

Fear will stop you. So will unhealthy stress caused by fear and panic. Change your thoughts and you will get rid of fear.

Fear not, little flock; for it is your Father's good pleasure to give you the kingdom.

(Luke 12:32)

The Church is visible, the Kingdom invisible. God has given you invisible money; invisible healing; invisible wealth. He is going to give you the wisdom and the ability to take it from the invisible and bring it into the visible.

It is God's good pleasure to give you the Kingdom! You cannot see the Kingdom, but you can see the Church. If you do not get into the Kingdom, you will never see what God wants you to see (His invisible Kingdom). The Church comes out of the Kingdom.

See your body totally healed. See yourself walking in the glory of God. See yourself wealthy, healthy and prosperous. See yourself going through menopause with no pause at all.

The Bible says that some people will see the Kingdom, but never enter it. It is time to enter it. When you enter the Kingdom, you take what you want...now, from the invisible and lock it into the visible.

Unhealthy stress can cause fear and panic about going into business. Trepidation about owning a business can cause you to become overwhelmed by the shock of making money. You are scared about the future, and have the fear of failure.

There is also a fear of success.

Open your eyes to see what others do not see.

I know some of you reading this book have a fear of failure and a fear of success. If you do not know what to do with your wealth, then give it to me and I will show you how to work it. The word "faith" is spelled "R-I-S-K"! If you operate in faith, you are taking a risk every time.

Declare now, "I am bringing to an end the being scared of the future. I am not going to have any fear of failure because there is no failure in God. I am in God, and there is no failure in me."

If you experience a temporary setback, just get back up and start all over again.

Say "good-bye" to the fear of uncertainty. Start moving out, but move out in wisdom.

Say "good-bye" to procrastination.

Hurdle Four:

The inability to enter your rest.

Many of you all are not restful people. You are everywhere, all over the map, into everything. You do not have any rest. That inability to enter your rest will stop the flow of money.

If you strain and labor to make money, you are not maximizing and putting the demand on the anointing of God. When you put a demand on God's anointing, Christ's anointing, the Holy Spirit's anointing, the Word's anointing, your struggle comes to an end, and you do not labor for money any more.

Money just comes your way.

There remaineth therefore a rest to the people of God. For he that is entered into his rest, he also hath ceased from his own works, as God did from his. Let us labour therefore to enter into that rest, lest any man fall after the same example of unbelief.
                                                              (Hebrews 4:9-11)

I want to enter into His rest. To enter into this repose position, I must be willing to fight this war from a position of rest, bringing every demon and evil spirit down out of my thought life. It serves no purpose to go into battle all hyped up and tense. God wants you to fight from a position of rest to win this war. You do not need to spend one moment in anxiety or tenseness, trying to make money happen for you.

And the peace of God, which passeth all understanding, shall keep your hearts and minds through Christ Jesus.
                                                              (Philippians 4:7)

Do you see it? God's Word is telling you to bring an end to the fighting and fussing. Take a deep breath. Inhale and exhale, and declare, "With Jesus, I am always in the fight." You can be in the midst of a war, right in the middle of difficulty, but know that you are going to win...from a position of rest!

Get into a position of rest fighting. The battle belongs to the Lord.

You can rest all night while others are doing illegal and immoral stuff, up all night shredding papers, trying to hide incriminating evidence. But when you are in your position of rest, nothing will steer you off your moral course. You will fight and defeat the enemy because you are going to be rested and they are going to be exhausted. Your rest will wear them down so you can come in and overtake them.

Thou wilt keep him in perfect peace, whose mind is stayed on thee: because he trusteth in thee.
                                                              (Isaiah 26:3)

In your rest, you will not experience mental illnesses, nervousness, migraines, headaches and irritability because your mind is fixed on Him. When you get in Jesus, craziness leaves. Schizophrenia leaves. Bi-polar leaves. Stop worrying about the state of your city...keep your mind on Jesus and the city problem will be solved.

> *Peace I leave with you, my peace I give unto you: not as the world giveth, give I unto you. Let not your heart be troubled, neither let it be afraid.*

(John 14:27)

Do not let your heart be troubled and you can avoid heart trouble, which comes from trouble not handled by faith.

Cast all cares upon Him because He cares for you.

Hurdle Five:

The inability to have a peaceful mind.

If you enter into your rest and can master the ability to not be anxious about making a living, juggling your time, or being anxious about a thousand other areas, then you can begin to operate in the wisdom of God.

There is a time for being with people, and a time to stay away from people so you can be in solitude with Him. Learn to shut the door for three hours (or whatever time you can), and ask your family to "Leave me alone, please." You do not need to be a nursing Mom or a "quality-time" Pop all the time. There is a time to father and a time to rest in God.

Take time each day, or at least three or four periods of time every week, to rest in God. Enjoy yourself. Take your shoes off. Read the Word. Rest your mind. Pray in tongues. Here me on this: *The inability to have a peaceful mind will stop money from flowing into your life*! An agitated mind, a racing mind that keeps you awake at night, has no ability to process financial goals.

We need His mind because ours aren't worth a quarter! Sometimes when our thoughts are wrong.

You have the wealth of God; His favor is upon you. Start enjoying life and the things of God. As you do, wealth will come to you. Here's three Scriptures that emphasize this process:

And the peace of God, which passeth all under-standing, shall keep your hearts and minds through Christ Jesus.

(Philippians 4:7)

Peace I leave with you, my peace I give unto you: not as the world giveth, give I unto you. Let not your heart be troubled, neither let it be afraid.

(John 14:27)

Of the increase of his government and peace there shall be no end, upon the throne of David, and upon his kingdom, to order it, and to establish it with judgment and with justice from henceforth even for ever. The zeal of the LORD of hosts will perform this.

(Isaiah 9:7)

When your mind is agitated, it will stop the flow of your money. Today, enter into the godly rest found in Hebrews 4:9-11:

There remaineth therefore a rest to the people of God. For he that is entered into his rest, he also hath ceased from his own works, as God did from his. Let us labour therefore to enter into that rest, lest any man fall after the same example of unbelief.

Start to experience a peaceable mind by keeping your thoughts on the Lord. Stop letting the enemy come in and get you disturbed and anxious. Declare today, "Wrong thoughts, you are a stumbling block to my anointing. Leave me in the Name of Jesus."

Fight to keep Satan's thoughts out of your mind. Satan's thoughts are usually your thoughts turned against you. Fight depression, oppressions, and foolish obsessions that spout lies like, "Nobody loves me or cares about me." That is from

241

your sick thoughts! Get that devil out of your thoughts by deciding to stay close to Jesus.

Fight to preserve and protect your mind. Before sickness manifests itself physically, it comes in through your mind, then works on your body.

You can possess all the money in the world, but if you are not healthy, you are not going to enjoy it. <u>You need both health and money</u>! Health without money still creates problems, as does money without health.

Many talk themselves out of the money anointing. Stop moaning and groaning and complaining all the time, talking about how sick you are, how hormonal you are. Nobody wants to hear about your sickness other than sick people. Instead, get your self healed and share the good news of your health!

Start declaring, "I will never be broke another day in my life. I will never be sick another day in my life." Saying it, especially out loud, builds your faith. Speak it out and refuse to be afraid of failure. The Bible says in Mark 11:23, that if we get sick we can be healed.

> *For verily I say unto you, That whosoever shall say unto this mountain, Be thou removed, and be thou cast into the sea; and shall not doubt in his heart, but shall believe that those things which he saith shall come to pass; he shall have whatsoever he saith.*

Hurdle Six:

The inability to profit from the Gospel preaching.

> *Let us therefore fear, lest, a promise being left us of entering into his rest, any of you should seem to come short of it. For unto us was the gospel preached, as well as unto them: but the word preached did not profit them, not being mixed with faith in them that heard it.*
>
> (Hebrews 4:1-2)

The Gospel must be mixed with faith. That's why everyone who hears the Gospel is not blessed by His Word. The preaching of the Word is not enough; each person must receive it by faith. We need every word that proceeds out of the mouth of God.

If you do not mix what I am sharing here with faith, you will be broke, poor, sick, uptight, and stressed out. You need faith to receive your anointing, to receive the Word, the Truth. God is a Spirit, and they who worship Him must worship Him in spirit and truth.

Some reading this book will be no better off after completing it, because they will fail to exercise their faith. They will continue to be sick and die before their time. They will remain broke because they will not mix these revelations with faith.

If you do not mix what is revealed here with faith, you are going to be worthless in the Body of Christ, and in this society. You will continue to complain, bellyache, and remain seriously uptight and frustrated all the time.

Hurdle Seven:

God is not going to deal with anybody who is indecisive.

You cannot come to God indecisive, not knowing what you want, because there are far too many problems to distract you if you do not remain decisive. Persecution, challenges and other problems can delay or slow your money if you are not decisive.

Make no mistake about it...you will suffer persecution and trials. The world does not want you to have abundance and wealth. If you do not have anything, you are not a threat, and they will not persecute you.

The inability to decisively face and handle persecution, challenges, and tough situations will delay your money because you will spend all your time dealing with the problems instead of focusing on the solutions.

Fruitful and Unfruitful Revelations

> *The sower soweth the word. And these are they by the way side, where the word is sown; but when they have heard, Satan cometh immediately, and taketh away the word that was sown in their hearts. And these are they likewise which are sown on stony ground; who, when they have heard the word, immediately receive it with gladness; And have no root in themselves, and so endure but for a time: afterward, when affliction or persecution ariseth for the word's sake, immediately they are offended. And these are they which are sown among thorns; such as hear the word, And the cares of this world, and the deceitfulness of riches, and the lusts of other things entering in, choke the word, and it becometh unfruitful. And these are they which are sown on good ground; such as hear the word, and receive it, and bring forth fruit, some thirty fold, some sixty, and some an hundred.*

> (Mark 4:14-20)

Notice in the above passage that there are three main responses and results to those who receive revelations from God's Word.

Response One:

The Word is Stolen

When attacked by wrong thoughts, this class of people allow the enemy to immediately steal the Word of God sown in their hearts.

Response Two:

The Word is sown on stony ground, and does not take permanent root.

In the second response, the Word is sown on stony ground. When the people first hear the Word, they receive it with gladness. They shout and holler, but because there is no deep root of the Word, these people go back to living lives of frustration and anger. They endure for a time, but when affliction and persecution arise, they repeat the same old pattern, getting hooked by the cares of the world. Deceitfulness, lust and other sins enter in, choking the Word until it becomes unfruitful.

Response Three:

The Word is sown in good ground and fruit is produced.

The third response is to hear the Word of God, and because the ground is good, the Word takes root and brings forth fruit! Some will bring forth thirty-fold, some sixty-fold, some a hundred-fold. I pray you are one who experiences this third response. If you are, then when you face persecution, you will respond in the godly ways.

My brethren, count it all joy when ye fall into divers temptations.

(James 1:2)

For the truth's sake, which dwelleth in us, and shall be with us for ever.

(2 John 1:2)

And there was great joy in that city.

(Acts 8:8)

His Lord said unto him, Well done, thou good and faithful servant: thou hast been faithful over a few things, I will make thee ruler over many things: enter thou into the joy of thy Lord. He also that had received two talents came and said, Lord, thou deliveredst unto me two talents: behold, I have gained two other talents beside them. His Lord said unto him, Well done, good and faithful servant; thou hast been faithful over a few things, I will make thee ruler over many things: enter thou into the joy of thy lord.

(Matthew 25:21-23)

Vow this minute to start walking in His Word, planted in good soil (that's you). Declare that you want to be a person who receives the Word with gladness and walks in the thirty-fold, sixty-fold, one hundred-fold, or the one thousand-fold anointing.

CHAPTER FOURTEEN

The Breakthrough Anointing is Here!

You are always going to have some challenges and problems in life, but the anointing destroys the yoke and burdens; it defeats the challenges. You will face difficulty, but through the anointing, you should not be in that problem for a long period of time.

There is not a single problem that will come up in your life that you cannot defeat through the anointing!

That's the attitude I apply in my own life.

No Distractions or Crazy People

Stay away from anything that depletes your anointing, such as family members who do not believe in God. They can rub off on you and deplete your anointing. Look at your life. If you are upset at the church, or burdened down with another's burden, or living a chaotic life, you need the anointing today. You need to receive and revive your spiritual oxygen supply.

Do not let anything separate you from the love of God.

Who shall separate us from the love of Christ? Shall tribulation, or distress, or persecution, or famine, or nakedness, or peril, or sword?

(Romans 8:35)

Nothing shall separate me from the love of Christ, the anointed One and His anointing!

Nothing!

No accident, no interruption, no financial challenge, no

sickness, no distraction...nothing shall not separate me from the Shemen anointing of Psalm 23 for this special money release, the special wealth release, the special abundance release.

> *Yea, though I walk through the valley of the shadow of death, I will fear no evil; For You are with me; Your rod and Your staff, they comfort me. You prepare a table before me in the presence of my enemies; You anoint my head with oil; My cup runs over.*
>
> (Psalm 23:4-5)

David was talking about God Himself...the God of Abraham, the El-Shaddai, Jehovah Jireh (my provision and provider). The word "oil" in this passage is the same word used for "Shemen." When you accept Christ as personal savior, this Shemen anointing is activated on your head. He anoints your head so you begin to see things you never were able to see before.

This anointing is also called "the revelation of God." He transforms your life, and you begin to see visions of God because your head has been anointed. This breakthrough revelation anointing includes four main visible areas you will experience: transformation, application, manifestation, and demonstration.

Visible Area One:
The Transformation of God

You need your brains, your intellect, your mind, your emotions anointed by God. You need to be running over with anointing, with the revelations of God.

Some people cannot see anything. They have no vision for business or economics, for international relations, or foreign affairs. The only vision they see is to live in a survival mode, barely getting long by living on "Begging Boulevard," right next to "Grumbling Alley."

Now is your time to overflow with the transformation power of God. "Transformation" means that, "I am changed by what I see." Of course, you can see something but not have the ability to change it. But when you become anointed by God, you can actually change what you see.

Many see things, but do not act.

Some see that they need to start a business, but they do not know how to put the business together; their mind must be transformed. You cannot think like a cocaine addict and run a business.

Visible Area Two:
The Manifestation of God

When your cup runs over, you are running over with the manifestations of God.

What are those manifestations?

Manifestations are things you can feel, touch, sense, put on right now.

When your money is manifested, it means that you have money now...you can touch it and circulate it.

Visible Area Three:
The Application of God

This means you know how to apply and appropriate your anointing on the earth.

You know how to help other people to get where they need to go in the Kingdom of God. You know how to help others apply the anointing to their businesses because you understand the principle of the application of God, which produces the wisdom of God you can share with others.

Visible Area Four:
The Demonstration of God

Application alone is not enough. You must be able to demonstrate how to walk in the anointing. You do not want to be talking loud, but saying nothing. You must demonstrate that you know how to apply the laws of God.

It is important that you be able to demonstrate to others what you can do, and what they can do, through the breakthrough anointing.

It is important that you say you are wealthy, but acting like you are wealthy is not enough. You must be able to demonstrate and walk in wealth, producing it in the earth. Remember you are the wealth of God.

Diversity of Kingdoms
for Financial Blessing

You can receive money from the animal kingdom, or any other kingdom. For example, veterinarians frequently develop new technologies which can then be transferred into helping humans. In the future, a Christian veterinarian may develop a method to put some sort of a new rubber hips on animals, which will then transfer into the human area. In the animal kingdom, the possibilities for money-making breakthrough are endless.

You can count on this...God will allow Christian veterinarians to extract money from the animal kingdom, from the cow kingdom, from the fish kingdom, from the horse kingdom. God is using the animal kingdom as one of His diverse methods to bless His people.

One person reading this book may be led to invest in Arabian horses. That person could make hundreds of thousands of dollars because they touched something in the animal kingdom, and through God's special anointing, money broke loose.

There is money to be made in the cat business, in the snake business. Forget about government hand outs, government peanut butter and government cheese. Let the wealth of the wicked eventually come into your hands through a diversity of kingdoms. The affirmative action days are over; you need to live by faith. Your affirmative action comes through the anointing!

You can make money in the animal kingdom, the mineral kingdom or the vegetation kingdom. You make money in plants and flowers. You can also make money in the human kingdom because the earth is the Lord's and the fullness thereof, so the wealth of the wicked will eventually come into our hands.

There's More Than Enough!

There is no scarcity.

We are not running out of gas and oil. If anybody is going to run out, it will be the wicked because I plan to have my gas, my house, my land, and my money.

There is no shortage, scarcity, or limitation on God. We are not going to limit the Holy One of Israel.

The Lord is my Shepherd and I shall not want.
(Psalm 23:1)

There are ideas and revelations that haven't even been discovered yet. There are cures that need to occur. Somebody is sitting on a revelation from God for a cancer cure, for a heart cure. It is time for us to walk in the release of His anointing for wealth and abundance.

There is money to be made even in the human, Satanic kingdom because the wealth of the wicked is laid up for the righteous. This world's system is of the devil, but God can give you the wisdom to use this world's system to your good, producing wealth and abundance.

Money is on its way. It has already been loosed in the Kingdom of God.

After Salvation, Experience Him in Your Life

There is more to God than getting saved. After salvation should come baptism and being filled with the Holy Ghost. Then, comes learning how to enter into the invisible Kingdom, the tabernacle of God. His Kingdom is not of this world, but He is in the midst of the world. We have a God Who sits high on the right hand of the Father with a scepter in His hand.

The days of playing church are over. When we come into the corporate church, seek and meet God, strive to feel Him, to see Him. The church needs to stop being a social club and start being kings and priests, destined to change society.

There is money in the invisible kingdom as you seek not to live in this earthy system and draw off the invisible kingdom.

Worship Him. Praise Him.

You can't praise Him when you are dead, so do it now! Look what the Amplified version says in Jeremiah 29:11:

For I know the thoughts and plans that I have for you, says the Lord, thoughts and plans for welfare and peace and not for evil, to give you hope in your final outcome.

The word "peace" here means "to prosper you." God wants us to prosper like a tree planted by the water. It is your heritage to prosper, to get ahead.

Walk in the Unseen

Remember, faith is the substance of things hoped for, the evidence of things not seen. While we look at the things

252

which are seen, we focus on the things not seen, because those are the eternal things.

What you see in the natural realm is not lasting nor eternal.

This is the day of the Lord, and we see through His Holy Spirit.

In the natural, your body may be twisted, your lungs may be bad, your kidneys may not be working. But you do not set your focus on what is wrong. Instead, you look at the kidney which is healed in the realm of the spirit.

> *God is a spirit and they that worship Him must worship Him in spirit and in truth.*
>
> (John 4:23)

The way you look right now is not how you will look in six months. Your bank account is not going to reflect in six months the meager balance it shows today. You are destined to experience a greater dimension, a greater healing, a greater anointing.

Dr. Leroy Thompson, in his book, *Money Cometh to the Body of Christ*, says that "your money is already here" because your money has already been loosed. Now, God is going to give you all the wisdom you need to extract it from the diverse kingdoms.

What you see right now is not the real world, but the invisible world where the spiritual action is going on. Money is being released to you in Jesus' Name.

> *Greater is He that is in us than he that is in the world.*
>
> (I John 4:4)

> *For I know the thoughts that I think toward you, says the LORD, thoughts of peace and not of evil, to give you a future and a hope.*
>
> (Jeremiah 29:11)

Whatever you have been thanking God for, whatever your long-range and short-range plans are, He is going to give you your expected end.

Poor No More

God is not trying to harm you or put you down. God doesn't make anyone sick. It would be a hypocritical God to bless you on one hand and make you sick on another. I would not serve a God that would do that to me. We don't serve a cruel God. Christ redeemed us from the curse of the law, from poverty, sickness and spiritual death. Poverty, sickness and death are not blessings from God. Christ the anointed one and His anointing have released us, have redeemed us from poverty, sickness and spiritual death.

Sickness is a curse.

Poverty is a curse.

You do not have to be poor anymore. You do not have to be broke another day. God sent His Son, Jesus, so you may become rich.

Yes, we are challenged to bless the poor and help them, but at the same time, we must declare, "I am poor no more. I used to be cursed and live in poverty, from one paycheck to the next. I blamed everybody for my condition until I found out that God is more than enough. I used to be poor, but I am poor no more."

Sick No More

Sickness is a curse.

Friends, when you are sick, you do not have any time for God, it is all about you and your sickness!

For many reading this book, these concepts may seem foreign and difficult to master, but you can if you yield yourself to the Holy Spirit. Maybe you are not there yet, but you can get there. Going by "feelings" is not faith. Living in denial is not faith. I have had stuff in my body that my faith got out of my body. As I went, I was healed.

Keep saying to your body, "With His stripes I am healed. I am delivered." Keep speaking out against the mountains in your life, telling them to be removed and cast into the sea.

Of course, the world will mock you, saying, "Look at that man. He is telling a lie." No, the man is using his faith! The day is going to come when he is able to lift his hands and declare, "I am healed."

God wants to place into our hands the wealth, health and abundance we need. He is not trying to harm us. He loves us.

For God so loved the world that He gave His only begotten son. That whosoever believes in Him shall not perish, but have everlasting life.

(John 3:16)

There is a hope and a future in God!

God made the end before He made the beginning. He already knows your end. The Bible says, *receiving the end of your faith* (1 Peter 1:9) to give you an expected end.

Receive now the end of your faith. Now healing, now abundance, now money. If it is not now, it will never be.

The anointing will cause your money to break out from every gate.

The breaker is come up before them: they have broken up, and have passed through the gate, and are gone out by it: and their king shall pass before them, and the LORD on the head of them.

(Micah 2:13)

Your money is breaking out from every kingdom. The animal kingdom, the vegetation kingdom, the Satanic kingdom, the human kingdom.

Receive your breakthrough anointing.

Become drunk with the anointing of God, filled with the Holy Spirit. Receive the anointing that will cause your money to break out of every gate. Your money will be shaken loose because of the anointing. The amplified version of Micah 2:13 reads:

The Breaker [the Messiah] will go up before them. They will break through, pass in through the gate and go out through it, and their King will pass on before them, the Lord at their head.

That banker who refuses to give you the loan will now have to deal with the anointing. Your house may have been hindered, but the mortgage company is going to have to let it go because the anointing has shown up.

The breakthrough anointing is here!

Say this prayer out loud:

Lord, thank You for breaking through and opening my spiritual eyes. My breakthrough is here. My anointing is here. I am a son of God. It is my right and heritage to receive this anointing and be healed, healthy and wealthy. I am like a tree planted by the water that brings forth fruit in its season. My leaves shall not wither, and whatsoever I do shall prosper. It is my right to break through and receive the breakthrough anointing.

Thank You, Jesus!
Amen.

Anointed Sons and Daughters in Marketplace Ministry

These sons and daughters of God are not just practicing signs and wonders in the marketplace, they are the new signs and wonders of God in the marketplace.

Behold, I and the children whom the Lord hath given me are for signs and for wonders in Israel form the Lord of hosts, which dwelleth in mount Zion.

(Isaiah 8:18)

The wealth transfer from the marketplace movement is occurring. The souls that will come from the workplace or marketplace is that new wealth. These souls are the new wealth of God in the marketplace.

Therefore said He unto them, The harvest truly is great, but the labourers are few: Pray ye therefore the Lord of the harvest, that He would send forth labourers into His harvest.

(Luke 10:2)

One of the major strategies of Releasing the Money Anointing is to help people understand and realize the anointing that they can have to obtain "surplus money" so that they can help promote the Gospel of the Kingdom through the earth, according to Matt. 24:14.

And this gospel of the kingdom shall be preached in all the world for a witness unto all nations; and then shall the end come.

We need billions and trillions of dollars to get the Word out all over the world about the Kingdom. ("Thy kingdom come, thy will be done.") God is not trying to destroy people in the world, he is trying to introduce His Kingdom to them. I pray that millions of people will be activated in the anointing of God as a result of this book.

Don't use your entire life trying to build a net worth. Use your time in generating money to bless others. Your net worth is determined by the degree of your anointing, not on the amount of money you have in the bank or in real estate investments.

You are the wealth of God! You are the investment of God in the earth.

When your human spirit has been regenerated by the Holy Spirit, and you walk in divine health, joy and peace, led by the Spirit of God, you are wealthy. Your anointing is a great plus for you to attract all you need in heaven and earth for yourself and others. Don't become too focused on your personal net worth. Focus on the anointing.

You can have money, materials and property, but not be anointed with divine health, prosperity, joy, peace and righteousness in the Holy Spirit. Use your anointing to obtain money to promote the Kingdom of God. You want to have a net worth full of the anointing.

It is time for you to get out into the workplace and marketplace and use your anointing.

The Anointing and the Manifestation of the Sons of God

This anointing is especially reserved for the sons of God.

There is a new wave of spiritual millionaires and billionaires emerging in America who will come from these new manifested sons of God. They will pop up all over the world during this decade.

How will you recognize these new, manifested sons of God?

They will be legitimate sons of God who have spent time under an earthly spiritual father. Jesus had a spiritual father and his name was Joseph. One of the purposes of a spiritual father is to bring the sons and daughters back to their heavenly Father's house. A second reason for the manifestation of the sons of God is to promote the expansion of the Kingdom of God in the earth. They will carry *a* certain signet (seal) on their lives such as the following (I first heard this taught by Brother Randy Shankle in Marshall, Texas):

　　1.　　The Signet of the Real.

2.   The Signet of Ownership.
3.   The Signet of Significance.
4.   The Signet of Approval.
5.   The Signet of Protection.
6.   The Signet of Restraint.
7.   The Signet of Sonship.

For I reckon that the sufferings of this present time are not worthy to be compared with the glory which shall be revealed in us. For the earnest expectation of the creature waiteth for the manifestation of the sons of God. For the creature was made subject to vanity, not willingly, but by reason of him who hath subjected the same in hope, Because the creature itself also shall be delivered from the bondage of corruption into the glorious liberty of the children of God.

(Romans 8:18-21)

"Where are the fathers?" is the cry in America. The Bible says there are many instructors but few fathers.

And will be a Father unto you, and ye shall be my sons and daughters, saith the Lord Almighty.

(II Cor. 6:18)

For though ye have ten thousand instructors in Christ, yet have ye not many fathers: for in Christ Jesus I have begotten you through the gospel. Wherefore I beseech you, be ye followers of me.

(I Cor. 4:15)

At the "Encampment" in Cincinnati, we are training sons and daughters how to come into their sonship, and how to appropriate the anointing of God in their lives with a view toward promoting the Kingdom.

As spiritual fathers, we must work in these sons of God the following:

The work of discipleship produces the right attitudes in a son or daughter. The right attitude is using the anointing relative to money and abundance.

The work of submission produces trustworthiness and eliminates independence and lawlessness. The anointing will not work in lawlessness.

The work of obedience helps a son or daughter to correct any disobedience prior to exercising the anointing.

The work of humility helps spiritual sons and daughters to eliminate pride and arrogance. Because you have this special anointing, you cannot afford to be arrogant.

The work of representation helps sons and daughters to eradicate the usurping and substitution of the Word of God. It asks the question, "Will you do what the anointing tells you without substitution of the Spirit message?"

The work of reflection teaches a son to understand how to handle the anointing of God effectively.

The work of maturation helps spiritual sons and daughters to move through the five Biblical stages of discipleship growth. The five words for this maturation are Biblical, Greek words:

1.   *Nepios* (babes and sucklings).

2.   *Padion* (infant).

3.   *Teknon* (teenagers).

4.   *Huios* (fully mature).

5.   *Pater* (father).

Some people are not ready to handle much material money until they go through the appropriate discipleship training.

(Note: For more detailed information on discipleship or sonship training, contact us at 1-513-681-3340 or 1-513-681-0424, or contact us on the worldwide web at www.churchincollegehill.org and give us your e-mail. We will respond.)

The Anointing and the Rule of God

The anointing of God is very powerful stuff, so you must handle it with care. Every person reading this book will have a measure of rule as it relates to the anointing in creating and generating spiritual money, transformative mind-money, or material money. A limited portion of the anointing will be measured out to you as you are in submission to God and the authorities over you. You will not be able to use your anointing to go beyond the lines or boundaries that God has given you. As long as you stay within your measure or line, you will have a pleasant outcome in using the anointing of God.

> *But we will not boast of things without our measure, but according to the measure of the rule which God hath distributed to us, a measure to reach even unto you.*
>
> (I Cor. 10:13)

> *The lines are fallen unto me in pleasant places; yea, I have a goodly heritage.*
>
> (Psalms 16:6)

There is no authority but from God (Who is directly over Jesus and the Holy Spirit). As you utilize the anointing of God, you must understand divine rule or authority.

God is a God of order.

Divine order or authority is designed for your covering or protection. You cannot use your anointing to promote self and independence, rebellion or arrogance, and retain the anointing. Even in heaven there is spiritual order. The "Shemen" anointing comes from being under the divine authority of the sovereign God of Abraham, Isaac and Jacob. The "Christos" anointing comes from being under the direct authority of Christ. The "Pneuma" anointing comes from being under the delegated authority of the Holy Spirit. The "Rhema" anointing comes from being under the authority of the Word of God. Jesus delegates all authority

261

to the sons of God, the elders, the Church and civil authority.

Order must be coupled with the anointing.

You must stay within your orderly arrangement to use the anointing effectively. You cannot use your anointing to rebuke governments, public officials, elders, or bishops, or disrespect anyone because just you are anointed. Civil authority is a delegated authority for your protection. You must submit yourself to the ordinances of God and man to be effective in the earth in appropriating your anointing.

Embrace order. Without it your prophetic anointing, teaching anointing, singing anointing, preaching anointing, healing anointing, or money anointing will shipwreck. It must be retained with order and character.

Let every soul be subject unto the higher powers. For there is no power but of God: the powers that be are ordained of God.

(Romans 13:1)

Apostolic Shift from Ministers to Sons

There is a new type of sons emerging who has not bowed down to the false god, Baal. These new sons will pop up all over America in the next ten years because they have been hidden in the house for this hour and day to release the money anointing in the earth. They are coming out from among the control and manipulation of various ministers. These sons will have an unction or anointing on their lives. They are smeared with a special endowment because they have spent time in the house of oil with their spiritual fathers training and developing them for this hour. These sons have been hidden in the house for this time to walk in financial wealth.

You cannot help but get oil all over your life after having been trained by a spiritual father in the house of oil. The earthly spiritual father's purpose is to get you to your heavenly Father so He can approve of you so you can rule in the earth with abundance. Then He will say, "My beloved son, in whom I am well pleased."

I am writing a book called *Cry Father* that will describe a comprehensive plan on how to train spiritual sons and daughters up in the house and the Kingdom of God. Cry Father will help churches in a positive perspective to move from a minister-ruled church or fellowship, to sons and daughters ruling and reigning together. Cry Father will also help parents in learning how to rear their children.

There is an anointing set aside for the spiritual sons and daughters. We train sons and daughters at the "Encampment" in Cincinnati on how to minister in the anointing, as well as a money anointing. Spiritual sons and daughters will be known in the earth because they will have the oil of anointing, the grease of the anointing, the liquid of the anointing upon their lives. Some insecure ministers will publicly attack these emerging sons and daughters because they will not have the ability to manipulate and control them. The anointing breaks manipulation and control, releasing sons and daughters of God so that God can rule and reign in the earth now.

There are five types of people Jesus dealt with:

1. **The Prosperity Group**

The crowd of five thousand followed Jesus because He could do something for them. This was the prosperity group. They follow because of what they can get: money, food or a miracle. We must minister to this group, but we cannot build on this group. They only show up on Sunday morning. These people see the Kingdom, but they will never enter the Kingdom of God on the earth.

The five thousand represents whatever number of people you have in your fellowship. Your five thousand may be a thousand people, or one hundred people. As long as you give these people fish and bread, they will follow you.

*Do ye not yet understand, neither remember the five
loaves of the five thousand, and how many basket ye
took up?*

(Matt. 16:9)

*And they that had eaten were about five thousand
men, beside women and children.*

(Matt. 14:21)

The five thousand will follow you as long as you can do
something for them. If you feed them and give them
prosperity teachings, they will follow you, but they will not
suffer with you. If one major storm hits your life, they are
gone. (Please receive this as a prophetic word.)

2.   People Who Promote their Ministries

The seventy that followed Jesus were people who
promoted their ministries. They were ministers who became
excited about signs, wonders and miracles, but their
character had not been developed. They had great
independent ministries, but very little character.

This group will see the Kingdom, but will not enter it on
earth. Every local fellowship has people who spend time
building their own ministries, but do little building up the
local church. You cannot build on these people. Many of
these local, independent ministers are unemployed and
under- employed because they don't won't work; they are
ministry-driven.

*And the seventy returned again with joy, saying,
Lord, even the devils are subject unto us through thy
name.*

(Luke 10:17)

The 70 were excited about their ministries, and caught
up only in self.

3.   Those Who Follow Jesus

The 12 are those who deny themselves, take up their cross and follow Jesus. Jesus had to get rid of the crowd and select twelve disciples so He could father them in His anointing.

The 12 are the people in the fellowship who you can build on by training them into character development with a view towards sonship.

There is a great apostolic shift that has occurred in the Body of Christ. There is a paradigm shift from ministers to sons. Because of this shift, that has been brought on by God Himself, we have a clash now between ministers and sons. Ministers versus sons. Some ministers do not want to give up the old ways of doing things (the old wineskins), still embracing the one-man rule or one-woman rule. But God is raising up His sons and daughters to rule together—a kingdom of priests, a plurality of sons and daughters who will rule and reign with their spiritual fathers in the earth.

The apostolic shift has brought about less emphasis on building man's ministry to a new emphasis on building up sons and daughters, taking them through the process of relationship building, discipleship training, fellowship building, sonship training, friendship training, and leadership building. It is time for the sons and daughters to claim their inheritance, to realize the money anointing.

The sons and daughters are the new buildings of God, the buildings we need to build. The sons of God are the carriers of the anointing and the presence of God, the new wineskins, the new money carriers of God in the earth.

They are the wealth of God.

And when he had called unto him his twelve disciples, he gave them power against unclean spirits, to cast them out, and to heal all manner of sickness and all manner of disease. Now the names of the twelve apostles are these; The first, Simon, who

is called Peter, and Andrew his brother; James the
son of Zebedee, and John his brother;

(Matt. 10:1-2)

God is bringing many sons unto glory. You may have
20,000 members in your fellowship, but your 12 disciples
may be only 300 people.

4.   The Three

Jesus had three men, Peter, James and John, who made
up the Apostolic Chamber of Christ. These are the people
in your inner circle; they are the closest to you. These are
the people who have suffered with you, the ones who have
experienced the baptism of suffering with you, the ones who
are hungry for Christ, the Anointed One, and His
Anointing.

These people have been anointed to be with you. You can
build with them. They realize that God is their source.
They are very resourceful sons of God. They know how to
use their anointing to create wealth, abundance and create
money for the Kingdom of God. These are people who will
pray with and for you.

And it came to pass about an eight days after these
sayings, he took Peter and John and James, and
went up into a mountain to pray.

(Luke 9:28)

5.   Then there is "the one."

His name was called John. You could always find John
laying on the breast of Jesus. This is the son who will die
with you, who will become your right hand person, and will
succeed you. This son has an intimate relationship with
you, and understands your humanity and deity. He has
been ordained to be with you for life. He is indeed a
manifested son of God who carries the Anointing and
presence of God. You really can trust him.

266

Apostolic Shift from Believer to Disciple

We thank God for raising up a new brand of elders, bishops, apostles, and prophets in this last decade who will be able to handle this big money anointing. The purpose of this raising up was for these men to father sons and daughters of God. Our emphasis must change from just covering churches to fathering sons and daughters of God. The next move of God is the manifestation of the sons of God, not the manifestation of corporate churches.

For the earnest expectation of the creature waitheth for the manifestation of the sons of God.

(Romans 8:19)

Sons in waiting are the next move of God until the return of Christ. They are destined to enjoy this invisible kingdom of wealth, abundance, prosperity, and money now! When God establishes His ultimate visible Kingdom, these manifested sons and daughters of God will rule and reign forever as prophets, priests, and kings.

Being "just a believer" or a churchgoer is not enough—you must manifest into a son of God. A believer should become a disciple in order to manifest as a son.

There is a clash, a war going on between believers versus disciples. The disciples are challenging believers, saying, "There is more to life than being a once-a-week churchgoer." Believers are frustrated all over the world because they are looking for oil in the wrong places. Believers are being challenged to go deeper in God; without this depth there will be more and more insecurity, fear and frustration.

Every believer must be transformed by this anointing in order to manifest as a son of God. In other words, a believer must go through a major metamorphosis of the anointing to come into sonship. That is why you need a spiritual father to assist you through your discipleship training. Too much time is being spent on covering "churches" instead of raising up sons and daughters of God in the house. The covering is for the sons and daughters of God. It is their protection.

Even a butterfly goes through four stages of metamorphosis:

1. First, the egg.
2. Second, a caterpillar (larva).
3. Third, a cocoon is formed (pupa).
4. Fourth, a butterfly (adult).

A believer must move from the Passover, which is salvation, to Pentecost, which is the baptism of the Holy Ghost, to the Tabernacles of God, which is the Kingdom of God, or the Holy of Holies. It is God's good pleasure to give His sons and daughters the Kingdom.

Fear not, little flock; for it is your Father's good pleasure to give you the kingdom.

(Luke 12:32)

There is a major shift in the earth from just preaching the Gospel of the Church to the Gospel of the Kingdom. The Church came out of the Kingdom, and not the other way around. Some apostles are rising up with the Gospel of the Kingdom. The Church was created to press out the Kingdom of God in the earth. Most churches are at a standstill because they do not know how to bring the church into the Kingdom. That's why each local fellowship should have an apostle to assist with the transition. The apostles can especially help with the transition of believers to disciples, and from ministers to sons.

And this gospel of the kingdom shall be preached in all the world for a witness unto all nations; and then shall the end come.

(Matt. 24:14)

The anointing is about multiplying, producing, and generating the purpose of God in your life. Sonship is a cry for the Father. There are billions of people throughout the world crying for their heavenly Father to manifest Himself in their lives. The cry is for the spirit of adoption, for the redemption of our bodies. The cry is to manifest as a son of God—now.

> *And if children, then heirs; heirs of God, and joint-heirs with Christ; if so be that we suffer with him, that we may be also glorified together.*
>
> (Romans 8:17-19)

There is a global cry, "Will someone show me the Father?"

> *Jesus saith unto him, Have I been so long time with you, and yet hast thou not known me, Philip? He that hath seen me hath seen the Father; and how sayest thou then, Shew us the Father:*
>
> (John 14:9)

Every son of God wants the Father to show up.

CHAPTER FIFTEEN

Receive Your Money Without Working Hard

I was recently talking with my Heavenly Father and received this revelation: "The Holy Ghost has set us up so that God things should not be hard."

The world will try and make these spiritual matters hard on you. But your life should not be hard from the standpoint that God has already given you all you need. Our Heavenly Father has given you a plan to receive money without working hard for it.

The world says, "You must work hard for your money."

No, you don't.

There are many people who do not work hard, yet still have plenty of money. Working hard will bring you bad health. God wants you to be a money master, a money machine, flowing with the ability to create wealth. You will not have to work hard for your money because money comes easy as a result of you being an heir of God. Healing comes as a result of you being an heir of God. **The anointing takes the hard work out of working hard so you can work smart.**

How Can This Happen?

How do you get money without working hard for it? Oh, you will need to do a little work, but you will not have to work hard. You will not need to stay up all night trying to figure out how to balance the books.

We are not going to work hard for our money because we have the anointing and power to create wealth and abundance through the rest of God.

Someone gave me a huge check the other day. Since this revelation has been fully birthed in my spirit, money just keeps flowing into my hands. I could not be writing about this anointing unless it was happening to me.

This is not a game. Once you receive this anointing that God has put on your life, and begin to activate it, you will see God open up doors for you, give you favor, and take you into places you have never been before. All because of the anointing, this mystery power.

Supernatural or Super Spiritual?

To activate the anointing, you need to understand some things about supernatural realm versus the super spiritual anointing.

The supernatural is the changing of the customary order of things. We frequently call the supernatural "a miracle." But there is something else that God has even better than the supernatural—the super spiritual anointing. Here's why it is better.

The supernatural is the suspension of the natural order of things, resulting in a miracle.

But you cannot live by miracles alone.

Supernatural and Super Spiritual

In the natural, a nearby landowner was not going to sell his land to our fellowship. He stoutly refused; the transaction would never happen. But the land became ours in the supernatural.

One day when I was teaching the School of the Prophets, I wrote a little letter and put the letter in the rocks in the building. I prayed, "Father God, right now in Jesus' Name, change the natural course, the customary order of things, and let this land come into our hands."

The landowner fully intended to build condos on the land. So I used my little seed faith and wrote a letter which I covered with dirt. I was walking in the supernatural and the super spiritual.

This book contains transformation revelations which will release the supernatural and the super spiritual into your life, into your finances.

You cannot live solely by miracles, constantly saying, "Lord, I need a miracle for my marriage, I need a miracle for my family." You are entitled to receive miracles as a heir of Jesus Christ, but not on a daily basis. However, you can live in the super spiritual anointing on a daily basis! With the super spiritual anointing, you will not need any miracles. The four major anointings of God which this entire book is based on is super spiritual.

The anointing will cause your money and your materials to flow. If you live and walk in the anointing of God, financial release and financial breakthroughs will occur all the time. The super natural is fine, but you want the super spiritual, which means you are going to receive from the anointing on a regular basis through you.

Not by might, not by power, but by My Spirit...
(Zechariah 4:6)

God is going to open up revelations so you can move into manifestation and transformation in your life. The anointing will cause money and materials to flow to you because you have stimulated your faith.

We cannot live by day-by-day miracles. We must live by faith. As we activate or faith, we activate the super spiritual. We do not look at things which are seen, but things which are unseen because they are eternal, of the Spirit.

My Visionary Leadership Room

I have turned our bedroom into a temporary apostolic visionary leadership room. On the wall I have a picture of the new apostolic encampment, a Bible training base scheduled to open in 2004. I have a picture of the new academic academy (yet to be built). I have a picture of people standing in line to enroll in the apostolic schools (over 3200 people have already registered since Sept 11, 2002). The purpose of these pictures? You must first see a vision before you can possess the vision!

I Have Made a Choice...

I have made a choice...

Not to live in the realm of solely the super natural.

I have made a choice...

To live in the realm of the super spiritual. The super spiritual is the Shemen anointing of God, the Christos anointing of Christ, the Pneuma anointing of the Holy Spirit, the Rhema anointing of the Word of God.

That is the super spiritual.

I have made a choice...

Not to just occupy on earth, but to also occupy the heavenlies.

I have made a choice... to live a balanced life in the heavens and in the earth.

The super spiritual is more powerful than dynamite, more powerful than just having a miracle. Miracles are great, but the super spiritual is greater. If you receive the super spiritual, you do not have to depend on changing the natural course or order of things all the time. You will walk in the new order, a new spirit, a new dimension all the time!

I have made a choice...

To receive my wealth, my abundance and my finances out of the realm of the super spiritual.

Now is God's time for you to come into the super spiritual. Receive your healing through the super spiritual. Receive your abundance, your money, through the super spiritual.

Stop dealing with the natural and start living in the Spirit.

We do not have to depend on the supernatural when we have the super spiritual.

You are healed by the super spiritual. Your money, wealth, and finances are being released through the super spiritual.

What is the super spiritual?

1. The Shemen anointing of God. It is God Himself involved in it. God Himself pouring out His anointing upon you.

2. It is the Christos anointing. It is Christ Himself. Christ the anointed One and His anointing that is involved in releasing this anointing in your life.

3. It is the Pneuma anointing where the Spirit will anoint you.

4. It is the Rhema anointing which comes by reading the anointed Word.

When you put all of these anointings together, God will give you wisdom beyond your days. You will be able to speak things that you never spoke before. He'll give you wisdom on how to get out of situations. He'll show you how to be on top and stay on top. He'll show you how to discern.

The Spirit will guide you and lead you into all truth.

It is all in the anointing!

The super spiritual anointing is activated by faith. Live by faith and activate the super spiritual. The super spiritual will become a common way of life for you. As you walk, you will change lives. As you move in your community, you change lives because you have an anointing. You become the life of God because you have been anointed by God with wisdom, to enter into a greater dimension of the Kingdom of God.

Make a decision today to live in the realm of the Spirit, the super spiritual, and it will become a common way of life. Money, wealth, health and abundance will flow to you all the time. Remember you are the wealth of God.

One of my daughters gave me a small amount of money. I said, "Thank you daughter," and she said, "It was just a small amount of money."

"No, it was not. That money was the initial seed of God, and it will come back to you a thousand times more."

That money she put in my hand was the initial seed that came from the anointing for her to release back for greater money and greater wealth. My daughter doesn't know this, but I have already saved thousands of dollars in her college education fund.

Vow to never live another day without being in the realm of the super-spiritual. Learn how to separate your humanity from your deity.

Start to walk in power with God. You are no greater than your Master. Enter into the realm of the super spiritual. Your war is not against flesh and blood. Put your demand on the super spiritual today. Receive your impartation today and declare, "I am not going to be like I've always been." Remember, if you keep on doing what you have always done, you will keep on getting what you have always got.

Lift the Name of Jesus until His joy comes into your life. As you do, you will move from the super natural into the super spiritual, releasing the money anointing.

CHAPTER SIXTEEN

Money Access
to Key People with Wisdom

A man's gift maketh room for him and bringeth him
before great men.

(Proverbs 18:16)

A man or woman's presents can give them access to great men. A man or woman's money can give them access to great people. A man or woman's money can give them access or exposure to great peoples' skill and knowledge.

Giving of gifts, money, rewards or presents to some key people is not bribery, but an opportunity to get access to a person with a view toward obtaining special information from that person, such as wisdom and good advice. We are not talking about violating any federal, state or city laws.

You may need key special information on scientific technology, medical data, computer technology, science, or religion. You may need access in the political world. Many times people give to political candidates to obtain access through their candidates to promote good government. This is fine as long as its not bribery or does not violate laws.

There are Biblical examples which demonstrate my point.

For example, the Queen of Sheba, seeking out answers and wisdom, brought gold to King Solomon. Her gift helped her to gain access to Solomon's wisdom regarding her questions.

And when the queen of Sheba heard of the fame of
Solomon, she came to prove Solomon with hard

questions at Jerusalem, with a very great company, and camels that bare spices, and gold in abundance, and precious stones: and when she was come to Solomon, she communed with him of all that was in her heart. And Solomon told her all her questions: and there was nothing hid from Solomon which he told her not. And when the queen of Sheba had seen the wisdom of Solomon, and the house that he built,
(II Chronicles 9:1-3)

Howbeit I believed not their words, until I came, and mine eyes had seen it: and, behold, the one half of the greatness of thy wisdom was not told me: for thou exceedest the fame that I heard.
(II Chronicles 9:6)

And she gave the king an hundred and twenty talents of gold, and of spices great abundance, and precious stones: neither was there any such spice as the queen of Sheba gave king Solomon.
(II Chronicles 9:9)

And king Solomon gave to the queen of Sheba all her desire, whatsoever she asked, beside that which she had brought unto the king. So she turned, and went away to her own land, she and her servants.
(11 Chronicles 9:12)

In another example, kings and governors brought gold and silver to Solomon.

Beside that which chapmen and merchants brought. And all the kings of Arabia and governors of the country brought gold and silver to Solomon.
(II Chronicles 9:14)

In yet another example, the Philippians gave money to Apostle Paul, which then provided them access, and in return, they were blessed.

Notwithstanding ye have well done, that ye did communicate with my affliction. Now ye Philippians know also, that in the beginning of the gospel, when I departed from Macedonia, no church communicated with me as concerning giving and receiving, but ye only. For even in Thessalonica ye sent once and again to my necessity. Not because I desire a gift: but I desire fruit that may abound to your account. But I have all, and abound: I am full, having received of Epaphroditus the things which were sent from you, an odour of a sweet smell, a sacrifice acceptable, well-pleasing to God.

(Philippians 4:14-18)

The Apostle Paul understood giving and receiving. He prayed the following blessing upon those who financially blessed him and his apostolic ministry.

But my God shall supply all your need according to his riches in glory by Christ Jesus.

(Philippians 4:19)

Apostolic means that Jesus, the sent One, shows up as Apostle to reflect the heavenly Father in the earth. Jesus gives the apostolic gifts to men to reflect the heavenly Father in the earth as spiritual fathers.

Financial giving is more for the giver because it is more blessed to give than to receive. The giver receives more from the giving than the person receiving the financial gift. Although many Christians do not realize this, financial giving is for you!

I have shewed you all things, how that so labouring ye ought to support the weak, and to remember the words of the Lord Jesus, how he said, It is more blessed to give than to receive.

(Acts 20:35)

Receive the Release of the Money Anointing

Receive the gift of giving or money now by activating the anointing of money at the highest spiritual level. The gift of giving or money can be imparted to you or transferred to you right now according to Romans 1:11:

For I long to see you, that I may impart unto you some spiritual gift, to the end ye may be established;

There are several other grace gifts that can be imparted to you also as in 1 Corinthians 12:4-11:

Now there are diversities of gifts, but the same Spirit. And there are differences of administrations, but the same Lord. And there are diversities of operations, but it is the same God which worketh all in all. But the manifestation of the Spirit is given to every man to profit withal. For to one is given by the Spirit the word of wisdom; to another the word of knowledge by the same Spirit; To another faith by the same Spirit; to another the gifts of healing by the same Spirit; To another the working of miracles; to another prophecy; to another discerning of spirits; to another divers kinds of tongues; to another the interpretation of tongues: But all these worketh that one and the selfsame Spirit, dividing to every man severally as he will.

The gift of giving or money can be stirred up in you, through the laying on of hands.

Wherefore I put thee in remembrance that thou stir up the gift of God, which is in thee by the putting on of my hands.

(II Timothy 1:6)

The **charismatic** gifts are a gratuity or endowment given from God, whether you are a Christian or not, because of His love for you. These gifts are grace gifts or charisma gifts activated by anointed men and women of God who can cause a release, impartation, or stirring up of these gifts in your life.

Receive right now the gift of money!

One of the purposes of *Releasing the Money Anointing* is to help you activate the anointing and gifts of God in your life.

Receive the reality of that money anointing right now!

EPILOGUE

A Radiated Word — Releasing the Money Anointing

By Coleen Winburn, wife of the author

Some will ask, "Why is it that I have never heard of Charles Winburn? Where has he been all of these years?" Others say to me, "I needed this message twenty years ago!"

Well, my husband has been hidden in the house of God for this season. For the last seventeen years, Charles has been going through intense discipleship training and character building under Randy Shankle, his spiritual father. I've seen great maturity in my husband as he has developed in character, word and spirit. God can trust him now with knowledge, wisdom, skill and money. I am always inspired by his prayerfulness and disciplined lifestyle. He devotes many hours to prayer and the study of God's Word. He truly represents a man who studies to show himself approved unto God in order to rightly divide the Word of Truth. He also is a man quick to admit his mistakes, ask for forgiveness, forgive others and stay in fellowship with others. He reminds me of David – a man after God's own heart, full of energy and the fire of the Holy Spirit. As my husband travels throughout the country to be an apostolic blessing to you, God can trust him to represent and demonstrate the love of God in spirit and in truth.

Releasing the Money Anointing is the result of many of the things he has learned and experienced during his intense discipleship training in his Father's house. I pray that you will allow God to use my husband to be a blessing to you. My husband is a living example of all that you read in this book.

Charles has been such a blessing to me, to our children, and to countless thousands of other people. *Releasing the Money Anointing* is a radiated word of God.

According to Matthew 4:4:

> *Man shall not live by bread alone; but by every word that proceedth out of the mouth of God.*

In other words, *Releasing the Money Anointing* is a proceeding word of God. The Word of God is the voice of God. The Bible is the voice of God. The Word is the bread of God. However, it is not all that God has to say about a situation, or all that God wants to speak to you. He wants to speak to you through both the Word and the Spirit.

Dr. Mark Hanby gives a good example of the proceeding voice of God versus the voice of God. As I paraphrase, he speaks of a passage in the Bible where God told Abraham to sacrifice Isaac. That was the voice of God. However, the proceeding voice of God was when he told Abraham not to kill Isaac, and a ram appeared in the thicket. If Abraham had killed Isaac immediately after he heard the voice of God, he would have missed the proceeding voice of God telling him not to kill the boy.

> *And the angel of the LORD called unto him out of heaven, and said, Abraham, Abraham: and he said, Here am I. And he said, Lay not thine hand upon the lad, neither do thou any thing unto him: for now I know that thou fearest God, seeing thou hast not withheld thy son, thine only son from me. And Abraham lifted up his eyes, and looked, and beheld behind him a ram caught in a thicket by his horns: and Abraham went and took the ram, and offered him up for a burnt offering in the stead of his son.*
>
> (Genesis 12:11-13)

Releasing the Money Anointing is a radiated or proceeding word of God in that God wants to say something to you

286

through the dimensions of the Spirit that He may not have told you through the Bible. Everything that God has to say to you is not in the Bible. The Bible does not contain all that God has said or will say to you presently or in the future. I believe the Bible to be the authoritative Word of God, but it is not all that God wants to say to you.

The radiated word is an activated word given from God through your spirit. This radiated word will become a live word through you. A radiated word brings the life of God, an utterance from the Spirit of God. *Releasing the Money Anointing* is a radiated word that God has for you that He was not able to give you until now. I have been married to Charles for twenty-four years. Because of the principles he teaches in this book, we have never experienced lack. These financial principles work for us, and God is no respecter of persons.

I would like to share one of Charles' secrets with you. Although he has the gift of money, he also has the gift of giving it away. The secret is that he always gives his surplus or abundance away (even if it means he has less) in order to bless others. When you understand this principle, you will not live in lack in any area of your life. God wants to give you a surplus of everything so you can give it away, just like Charles.

Finally, God does not want to speak to you just through the letter or scripture, but through the Spirit.

> *Who also hath made us able ministers of the new testament; not of the letter, but of the spirit: for the letter killeth, but the spirit giveth life.*
> (II Corinthians 3:6)

God wants to speak to you now through both the Word and the Spirit.

> *But the hour cometh, and now is, when the true worshippers shall worship the Father in spirit and in truth: for the Father seeketh such to worship him.*

God is a Spirit: and they that worship him must worship him in spirit and in truth.

(John 4:23-24)

Your heavenly Father wants to remarry both the Word and the Spirit in your life through the radiated word. Open your heart to receive the *Releasing of the Money Anointing*.

Coleen D. Winburn